Slip-Ups and The Dangerous Mind

*Seeing Though and Living
Beyond the Psychopath*

Wolf Thiessen, Ph.D.

Copyright © 2012 Wolf Thiessen, Ph.D.

All rights reserved.

ISBN: 1470047845

ISBN 13:   9781470047849

The Vision

Slip-ups and The Dangerous Mind:
Seeing Through and Living Beyond the Psychopath

Wolf Thiessen, Ph.D.

Then you will know the truth, and the truth will set you free.
BIBLE: JOHN 1:14

We share a large part of our lives with psychopaths that are often charming but ultimately despotic. They infiltrate every corner of our lives, have little empathy for our feelings, lie, engage in risky behaviors, cheat, manipulate our behavior, and show no remorse for their destructive urges.

Yet, they are difficult to identify, as they fly false flags of charm, beneficence, camaraderie, and good intent. Born on the ancient fields of evolutionary battle, and pushed forward by opportunities, they roam the earth at the expense of others. Their true malicious intents lay hidden.

Common science informs us that psychopaths represent about one or two percent of the male and female population, but that estimate, be it bad, is consistently lower than the data suggest. In fact, the prevalence may reach as high as fifteen percent, far higher than rates for heart attack, cancer, or cognitive or behavioral deviations. If you encounter 1000 individuals a day, at school, in stores, and on the street, 150 of them will be psychopathic. Not only do innate qualities assure high rates of psychopathy, but environmental contingencies, demographic factors, mob interactions, and inclinations toward criminality cause the psychopath to flower. We analyze the psychopathic flexibility from the street con game, among your friends and relatives, to the corporate boardroom and high political office.

The tasks laid out in this short book are to (1) give the reader the edge in identifying the male and female psychopath, (2) learn to understand his or her underlying motivations, (3) get out of harm's way, and (4) counteract negative influences of psychopathy.

You will learn how psychopaths think, how to detect when they lie, how to analyze their unusual linguistic behaviors, and even, in some cases, how to read their body language. The lessons taught here will help you avoid damaging sexual encounters, and devastating social and business interactions. The strategies are invaluable for giving you the edge to defeat psychopathic insults on your life, and increase your short and long-term prosperity.

In-depth searches for "Mr. Bad" are found on the author's website, *Dark Side of the Brain* (www.darksideofthebrain.com) and in his weekly blog from the same website. Wolf Thiessen can be contacted at neves82884@my-packs.net, Face Book, and Twitter.

The Author

Wolf (Del) Thiessen is a writer and researcher. He began his academic career at Denver University, received his B.A. degree at San Jose State College (now SJS University) and earned his Ph.D. degree at the University of California in Berkeley. He researched alcohol responses at Scripps Clinic and Research Foundation in La Jolla and investigated animal and human social behavior in the Department of Psychology at the University of Texas at Austin. He has published nine books and over 250 research articles. At the University of Texas Dr. Thiessen studied the evolutionary mechanisms of animal and human social behavior. Dr. Thiessen is Professor Emeritus with interests in human psychopathology, history, literature, and evolutionary psychology. His hobbies include playing blues harmonica (somehow acquiring the name Wolf), writing fiction, inventing magic tricks, playing billiards, and interacting with barnyard animals. He can be contacted at

neves82884@mypacks.net

Dedication

I wrote this book with my wife, Denise Stokes on my mind, and my good friend Jo Ann Wilder. Both contributed to my thought and both accepted my faults.

Table of Content

Acknowledgement	xi
The Blurry Edge	1
The Grand Prix Circuit And Visions Of Death	9
Sociological Psychopathy	23
Cauldron Of Psychopathic Spriit	33
Psychopath Theater	47
Trouble At home And In The Office	59
Identifying The Psychopath	67
Profit And Loss On A Giganic Scale	85
Blacker Than Black	93
The Discontent Of Knowing	107

Aknowledgement

The true pioneers that shaped the study of human psychopathy and influenced everything I say in this book include H. Checkley who in the 1940's and 1950's built the database for recognizing variations in psychopathic behavior, Robert Hare who devised the Psychopathy Checklist PLC-R and established a four-factor system of classification of psychopathic behaviors, Marvin Zuckerman who gave us decades of insights into sensation-seekers and developed primary scales for measuring their behaviors, as with the Sensation Seeking Scale (SSS-V), Antonio Damasio who knows more than just about anyone about the frontal lobe contribution to the identity of the self and the slippage into psychopathy, Kent Kiehl for critical and bold brain imaging studies implicating multiple pathways that are the infrastructures of psychopathy, many behavior geneticists who laid the foundation for linking DNA variations to evolution and deviant behavior, E.O. Wilson who brought together animal and human studies of behavior in the powerful book, *Sociobiology*, and who planted the seeds for the newer discipline of Evolutionary Psychology, William Sheldon who demonstrated the relations among body build and fundamental qualities of normal and psychopathic behavior, opening critical investigations in neuroendocrine regulators, and James Q. Wilson, Richard J. Herrnstein, and Charles Murray , and Richard Lynn and Philippe Rushton who outlined the critical genetic and environmental components of human intelligence and socio-economic features of criminal and non-criminal behavior. More specific to our intents is a seminal report by the late Linda Mealey on the sociobiology of sociopathy, a must-read for the understanding of the psychological world of the psychopath.

The Blurry Edge

Free yourself from psychopaths:
One small step for man, One giant leap for mankind

I have a double mission that guided my first thoughts for this short book. The first is to highlight the characteristics of a psychopath. The second is to explain how to identify and avoid the irresponsible psychopath or how to outwit him or her and live a more prosperous and pleasant life. It may be more complicated than that, but we can start with that mission and see if it can be achieved.

If we could adopt such strategies things might be better. We are surrounded by dangerous thugs that somehow infiltrate every corner of our lives: they weasel into our love affairs, our jobs, our business dealings, our politics, and envelop us in unintended conflicts with swindlers, con men and women, deep dish liars, narcissistic want-a bes, and callous robbers not to mention the alleged naïve persuaders, cognitively variable, and witless. It would be great if we could side-step psychopaths altogether, but losing our concentration we fall into their hands. Dealing with one is bad enough, as Shakespeare knew, but the planet is heavily seeded with psychopathic energy.

> *"You are polluted with your lusts, stained with the guiltless blood of innocents, corrupt and tainted with a thousand vices."*
> SHAKESPEARE *HENRY VI*

Whatever defenses you muster, you can't depend on the data presented. The statistics and descriptions on the numbers and characteristics of psychopaths are incredibly poor and should be disregarded. Probably society's perception of psychopathy is too narrow. Our health specialists and scientists tell us that about one percent of the male population is psychopathic and about half that number of females. That would be bad enough, if true, but it is far worse than that. Our advantage will come only if we admit that our lives are filled by psychopaths, all with self-centered and narcissistic messages of privilege. We look at the worst cases and what the professionals tell us, and use them as our measure of truth. Forget it; we need a new perspective, even if it's colored in dark paints.

The Enemies of Society

In addition to the typical psychopath that draws our attention, there are the general sensation seekers who engage in extreme sports, those who drive criminally fast, fill their brains with hallucinogens, stimulants, downers, horror movies, irascible conduct, promiscuity, and general indifference. They can profoundly affect our lives. Others we need to put on our short list are corrupt politicians, pedophiles, murderers, obsessive-compulsive sorts, suicide bombers, potentially explosive bipolar sickos, psychotic disturbers of the peace and public safety, attention deficit disordered this and that, antisocial personalities, ideological nitwits, aggressive maniacs that will beat you to a pulp and murder you just for looking them in the eyes, trained assassins and hit men, unstable parents who lock their children in basements, closets, and cages, uncategorized spooky freaks, cult leaders, mass murders, Mafia types, racists, thieves, rapists, arsonists, corrupt politicians and the just plain stupid. To a degree they carry a psychopathic taint.

All of these characters may, and often do, share traits with our views of classic psychopaths. They may be grandiose, completely lack empathy with those they overrun or overpower, show no guilt or remorse for their behaviors, endanger themselves and others by extreme forms of risk-taking, are aggressive, feel entitled to take what they want, seek all kinds of power over others, find criminal advantage, and reject the notion that you should have privileges, property, and money they don't have or won't work for. These are in part defining characteristics of the psychopath, but are often overlooked. They seem to apply to much wider populations than most medical and scientific professionals suggest. All of these rainbow folks can be gathered up in a general category of "hopeless and dangerous."

Collective Psychopathy

We obviously have a problem of classification, and I've only referred to deviancy among individuals; the problems of classification and explanation of psychopathy go far beyond the individual. We intuitively know that, but we rarely come to grips with the implications. I'm talking about a form of sociological psychopathy that arises not just among individuals (micro psychopathy) but a form that is derived from our culture (macro psychopathy) as well as where we are on the demographic pyramid. This collective or cultural form of psychopathic behavior is ultimately more widespread and dangerous than that bubbling within the individual. It's when likeminded psychopaths ban together in common purpose that things get hot for everyone.

For example, psychologist Martha Stout writing in her book, *The Sociopath Next Door,* (Broadway Books, 2005) points out that Asian cultures exhibit antisocial personality disorders ranging from 0.03 to 0.14 percent of their populations, whereas Western cultures show an average of 4.0 percent of the same deviations. In other words, Western cultures demonstrate up to 133 percent more antisocial disorders than Asian cultures and about four times more of these behaviors than statisticians attribute to our own culture. The cultural differences are manifestly critical for our understanding of psychopathic behaviors, as they can be more intrusive than individual behaviors. We don't know why these differences exist — they may be genetic or environmental in nature — but they could account for the largest share of the total variation in the deviant traits.

Associated with the cultural variations in psychopathic behaviors are demographic forces that push conflicts, revolutions, and war either up or down. Demographers Christian Mesquida and Neil Weiner center their attention on male warlike aggression and show a widespread relation between conflict behaviors (everything from competition with peers to protests, rob mobs, revolutions and wars) and national male age ratio (MAR), defined as the number of men aged 15 to 29 years of age, relative to males aged 30 and older. In other words, conflicts including wars between nations, civil wars, and other forms of aggressive behavior are higher in frequency among populations that have a higher ratio of younger to older males. Using the male ratio is consistent with the data showing that young males, and not females or older males, most often commit aggressive and antisocial acts. It is also consistent with the findings that it is generally young males who are sensation seekers, psychopaths, street protesters, terrorists, and the movers of cultural reform, not females, not fathers, not old guys wondering if they can ever retire.

Mesquida and Weiner publishing in *Politics and the Life Sciences* (September, 1999), illustrate data to confirm this relationship. In 153 countries and among 12 tribal societies there are clear relations between the severity of conflict and the proportion of young males (MAR) in these populations. As MAR approaches and exceeds 50 percent, national conflict increases. As MAR goes down with aging populations those conflicts subside. The overall correlation between extreme conflict and male age ratio is around 0.76, which is almost out of sight for sociological data. A correlation of .76 means that nearly 60 percent of the action is related to the male bulge and 40 percent to other variables that we know less about. Are the effects in part genetic? You bet: maleness is genetic, general male aggression and competition for mating are genetic, and age related changes in violence are genetic. The environment is also significant, exaggerating or diminishing the genetic impact on behavior.

The relative potential for serious outbreaks of conflict is evident in the Middle East and also Africa, with high proportions of young males, but is less in Western countries that are in transition to older populations. Numbers that summarize population events can mean a lot, and they tend to reflect the general case. They express the probability that murder, war, revolutions, and terror will envelop a nation and perhaps bring down civilization. There are armies of psychopaths living under volatile conditions, ready to strike.

Risk of Violence for World Countries: Median Age for Males *

TEN HIGHEST COUNTRIES		TEN LOWEST RISK COUNTRIES		SPECIAL INTEREST COUNTRIES	
Country	Age	Country	Age	Country	Age
Uganda	14.9	Greece	41.1	World	28.4
Niger	15.0	Finland	40.7	United States	36.8
Mali	15.8	Austria	41.5	China	36.8
Yemen	16.8	Guernsey	41.8	United Emirates	30.2
Congo Republic	16.3	Hong Kong	42.4	Israel	29.3
Chad	15.5	Jersey	42.5	Iran	27.6
Burundi	16.6	Germany	42.3	Panama	27.2
Bukina Faso	16.6	Italy	43.0	Mexico	26.7
Ethiopia	16.5	Japan	42.9	India	25.9
Malawi	17.2	Monaco	48.0	Libya	24.2
				Egypt	24.0
				Jordan	21.8
				Saudi Arabia	21.6
High Risk Age	14.9 – 16.5			Syria	21.5
Low Risk Age:	41.1 – 48.0			Pakistan	21.2
Medium Risk Age:	16.6 – 41.0			Kenya	18.8
				Afghanistan	18.0
				Yemen	16.4
				Spain	40.1

* "Median" age is the age where 50% of the male population is below that number, and where 50% of the male population is higher than that number. Generally a "median score" correlates positively with an "average score."

Uganda, with a male median age of 14.9, thus a country of young males, is more likely to engage in violent behaviors in the future than Japan, with a male median age of 42.9, a nation of old males. The United States has a fairly high age for males, 36.8, associated with relatively low risk for violence, but that may be changing because of demographic shifts toward more young males as mass immigration continues.

Other young male hotspots include Paraguay, Venezuela, Southern Sudan, and Brazil. Almost no one considers the fact that most group confrontations — Islamic provocations, political assaults, urban riots, military incursions, protests against losses of government welfare, overthrow of governments, and general terrorism are perpetuated by young males with high testosterone levels. The most dangerous are surplus young males that are not chosen by marriage-age females, males in poverty, males without hope for the future, except, perhaps, by adopting more aggressive short-term mating styles, or aligning themselves with permissive governments. We might properly refer to MAR as a measure of population testosterone and sensation seeking.

In a critical issue of *Science* on the young and the restless, Jack Goldstone, a political scientist at George Mason University in Arlington, Virginia, summarizes the importance of demographic changes.

> *"In the end," Goldstone says, "demography has turned out to be a better tool for analysis than any alternatives — and the youth bulge theory works more than it fails." In terms of broad probabilities," He says, "Demography tells you almost everything you ought to know."*
> SCIENCE, VOL. 333, JULY 29, 2011

Going From Here

This "handbook for survival" is dedicated to the practitioner of common sense who wants to beat the odds when staring into the eyes of someone who just doesn't give a damn whether you are alive or dead. This is the most pointed insult we must get use to and our first line of defense. I will attempt to minimize your "slip-ups" when challenged by the dangerous mind.

Not caring a whit what others want is the biggest advantage the psychopath has. Callous to the core and without empathy, the hard-core psychopath is operating without regard to social values or reservations. "He/she" (my contraction of "he" and "she" in order to avoid constant awkward grammar) is without empathy, and is therefore a whisper away from evil. Moreover, dissatisfied psychopaths are likely to gang up on us, spreading their venom widely and for longer periods of time, especially when encouraged by psychopathic leaders and media hounds that thrive on chaos.

At the micro level of the individual, he/she has no compunction about lying, stealing, or screwing you over. Moreover, he/she likes it even better if you are beguiled by deception, charm, and big promises. Loving them for their colorful presentations makes taking advantage of you even easier. They draw upon your trust, smile (at your naiveté?), promise you anything you want, and then sock it to you.

No goal is too big or too little for them to be insincere. And, we just don't get it when it happens. It is unbelievable that anyone could be so narcissistic and cold that they actually care nothing about you or your values. But how could they? They honestly don't feel those values; they can only pretend.

A common outcome is exemplified by a hapless owner of a motor home who was nearly ruined by Charlie Smith (actual name), a slick con man from the Midwest, who befriended the owner, only to bilk him out of his motor home with a fraudulent certified check for top price. The unfortunate man, now on foot, was devastated.

> *"How could he do that to me? He was always so warm, and we became friends. How could he do that to a friend?"*

If you have a sense of morality and live according to convention, you probably believe that your friends and associates share much of that same morality, and they probably do. But that is not how the human pie is cut by a psychopath – the pie comes in unequal slices and you may end up with the smallest piece. In a sense, you can be trapped by the psychopath because of your expectations of morality in other people.

Given that warning for starters, here is my agenda for this book. It is intended to help you get and keep your share of the pie. I'll begin by talking about sensation seeking and how it blends over into psychopathy. Sensation seeking is a philosophical killer and illustrates the possible basis of psychopathic motivations. I will go on to give you clues about the detection and destruction of the psychopathic influence. I'll give you ways to test for psychopathy mano y mano, including how to detect lying, exaggerated narcissism, lack of empathy, strange patterns of speech, deviant body language, duplicity in reciprocal interactions, and possible criminal behavior. The signals are often clear. The hard part is not being sucked in by a snake's arresting charm.

I will also discuss more formal measures of psychopathy, such as checklists and other methods of evaluation, and explain their value and drawbacks. Mainly I bring these methods and perspectives to your attention in order to increase your information about psychopaths and their extreme behaviors. There are about 20 related traits that give a fair representation of the psychopathic mind. This will be a good place to launch the discussion of the evolutionary, genetic, and neurophysiological imperatives that fuel the infrastructure of the behaviors we encounter. There are some new and exciting findings that are giving us insights into the causes of psychopathy and how we may be able to mitigate some traits of the psychopath.

I'll discuss more about the macro or cultural side of psychopathy that is now spinning its way through the world, including the United States. It, too, is easy to detect, but far more difficult to deal with. But there are ways. In all, I am attempting to introduce you to new considerations of an old problem and how you can benefit from understanding the mainsprings of psychopathy.

I will try to bring the information home by showing you illustrations of how the psychopath operates in the board room, the bedroom, on the job, and on the street. My intent is not to scare you but to help you build a shield against the most egregious assaults that come your way. The difficulties are compounded by the increasing number of psychopaths that knock on our doors.

Ignoring all the low estimates of the number of psychopaths, my personal estimate is that about 15 percent of the he/she population has medium to high psychopathic impulses, making them perhaps the most widespread deviations on earth, overshadowing every other disease condition, developmental and social problems, and criminal activity that one can imagine. Thus, in the United States alone there are probably 18 million individuals with significant psychopathic tendencies surrounding you. By chance alone, then, if you encounter 1000 people each day at stop lights, grocery stores, on internet, in business, at school, or at home, you will come within a breath of approximately 150 individuals with relatively high levels of psychopathy. Surprised? No wonder we need to be on guard. Regardless of the immensity of the problems we still can do much to immunize ourselves against psychopathic attacks.

THE GRAND PRIX CIRCUIT AND VISIONS OF DEATH

Let us have wine and women, mirth and laughter,
Sermons and soda-water the day after.

Lord Byron

Sensation Seeking

Klaus Manhart writing for *Scientific American* in 2005 reflected on the 1950s movie *Rebel Without a Cause* starring James Dean to point out the fatal attraction of sensation seeking:

"The two empty cars sit idling, side by side. Jim and Buzz each get into their vehicles, close the doors and push their gas pedals to the floor, racing headlong toward the edge of the cliff: the canyon below comes into view – they should each leap from their driver's seats before their cars vault into the abyss, but the first one to bail out loses. At the last possible moment Jim throws open his door and dives out onto the ground. Buzz waits too long and plummets over the edge to certain death."

Sensation Seeking Finds a Home

James Dean showed us the rebel within us, and provoked our imagination. In 1955 following his fast string of famous movies Dean began racing cars in the Palm Springs Road Races, the Minter Field Bakersfield Race and the Santa Barbara Road Race. Driving, instead of transporting his new Porsche 550 Silver Spyder on the way to a road race in Salinas, he crashed into another car nearly head on and died. From a short distance the wreck looked like grilled barbecue. The car was pulled around the country to show what could happen to a speeder. Later while on tour the car vanished and a million dollars was offered to anyone producing the car. The money was never claimed. Dean became a cult celebrity in death and even today that's his reputation.

About this same time British psychologist Hans J. Eysenck developed a scale for the behavior of extraversion and other personality traits, concluding that risk-taking was one of the best predictors of extraversion. Risk-taking and extraversion were now holding hands. Around the same time Marvin Zuckerman at the University of Delaware introduced us to the extreme seekers of thrills and near death. Suddenly we were surrounded with new ideas about personality and human nature.

The finishing touch on this stunning body of information and discoveries was announced by Hersey Cleckley — again in the early 1950s — that there is a cluster of 16 psychopathic traits that includes an uncontrollable narcissism called "Inadequately motivated anti-social behavior" that shows early onset, little change over time, and is found in a wide range of people. The trait of narcissism was associated with repeated risk-taking. Cleckley's rendition of psychopathy is repeated below.

Cleckley's 1950 Criteria for Psychopathy

1. Superficial charm and good intelligence.
2. Absence of delusions and other signs of irrational thinking.
3. Absence of nervousness.
4. Unreliability.
5. Untruthfulness and insincerity.
6. Lack of remorse or shame.
7. Inadequately motivated anti-social behavior.

8. Pathological egocentricity; incapacity for love.
9. Poor judgment and failure to learn by experience.
10. General poverty in major affective reactions.
11. Specific loss of insight.
12. Unresponsiveness to general interpersonal relations.
13. Fantastic and uninviting behavior with drink and sometimes without.
14. Suicide rarely carried out.
15. Sex life impersonal, trivial, and poorly integrated.
16. Failure to follow any life plan.

His massive summary of his work can be downloaded free from the internet. Cleckley is best known for his work on multiple personalities with Corbett Thigpen producing the 1957 movie *The Three Faces of Eve.*" *Cleckley died in 1984.* Indeed, as he believed, psychopaths often appear to have alternate lifestyles and identity. The strict definition of sensation seeking is seen in the table below.

Summary of Sensation Seeking:
The Scale and Implications *

Sensation seeking is the tendency to pursue novel, risky and stimulating experiences. Individuals show preferences for change, unusual situations, and uninhibited, unpredictable, extraverted, and risky behaviors.

Sensation Seeking Scale

The directions for filling out the scale are from Marvin Zuckerman (2007). I present only a few sample statements from the scale of 40 statements.

1. A. I like "wild" uninhibited parties
   B. I prefer quiet parties with good conversation

2. A. There are some movies I enjoy seeing a second or even a third time
   B. I can't stand watching a movie I've seen before

3. A. I often wish I could be a mountain climber
   B. I can't understand people who risk their necks climbing mountains

The likely responses of a sensation seeker for the above choices are A, B, and A.

Four Factors Have Been Isolated

1. Thrill and adventure
2. Experience seeking
3. Disinhibition
4. Boredom susceptibility

Characteristics of the Sensation Seeker (SS)

1. Males seek sensations more than females.
2. SS is age-dependent, stabilizing between the ages of 16 and 20 and decreasing thereafter.
3. Racial differences are small.
4. SS are seen as more attractive by others, including the opposite sex.
5. SS are likely to have the following personality traits: extraverted, non-conformist, impulsive more masculine (males), risk taker, not mentally abnormal, open to more sexual experiences, often uses alcohol and other drugs, gamble more, go for extreme sports, tolerate more pain, prefer complex stimuli in art, are more cognitively complex, interested in "outgoing" professions, have more vivid images, dreams, and daydreams, have higher levels of reproductive hormones, lower monoamine oxidase (MAO) activity, and thus higher brain dopamine levels.
6. Sensation seekers show heritable genetic variation at the level of 50 to 60 percent.
7. Sensation seeking may be a subclinical psychopathic complex of traits.

*Based on (1) Zuckerman, M. (2007). Sensation Seeking and Risky Behavior. Washington: American Psychological Association, (2) Kopeikin, H.S. Sensation seeking. www.psych.ucsb.edu/-kopeikin/ssinfo.htm.

Sensation seeking is often found in psychopaths, but they are not synonymous. James Dean may have been a little spooky, but he wasn't a hard-core psychopath, as I earlier suspected. Rather, he was a tough energetic risk-taker, with money and the motivation to go beyond the possible. Psychopaths do seek stimulation and take great risks, but so do non-psychopaths. At some level it is just another evolved human trait. However, it might be accurate to suggest that there is a continuum among personality forms, or at least patches of common traits, including psychopathic-like traits. James Dean and other drivers share a "soft" core of psychopathy that lies just below the defining characteristics of the typical psychopath.

Sensation Seekers Offer No Apologies

Tucked away on the Fox News website is a story that shouts there is nothing more incredible than the truth. A group of Australian senior citizens suffering from Parkinson's disease is launching a legal suit against drug companies Pfizer Australia and Aspen Pharmacure that produce the anti-Parkinson drugs Calaser and Permax, respectively, claiming that the drugs cause compulsive gambling and addiction to pornography.

Both Calaser and Permax are classified as "dopamine agonists," that mimic the action of dopamine in the central nervous system, thus counteracting the deficiency related to Parkinson's disease. Dopamine agonists that activate two quite specific behavioral syndromes are a stunning and unexpected clinical breakthrough, if true, that is. The images are sharp and even amusing.

We might believe that the story was someone's idea of a joke, that is, until someone distributed an article about the Mayo Clinic, discussing the same effects of dopamine mimics: Erin Richards begins the article this way:

> *"According to a new study published by the Mayo Clinic, patients with Parkinson disease (PD) have another problem to deal with. Researchers have found that one in six patients taking therapeutic doses of certain prescription drugs for management of PD have developed troubling behavioral symptoms. The most problematic symptoms include compulsive gambling and hyper sexuality."*

Slip-Ups and The Dangerous Mind

Drugs like Pramipexole and Ropinirole are implicated, adding to the list of drugs like cocaine, amphetamine, and nicotine, as well as Calaser and Permax that can stimulate the release of dopamine or substitute for dopamine in the central nervous system to halt Parkinson disease. We can now see the basis for the legal action. Dopamine is a powerful motivator of risk-taking even among those that have never had a desire for sensation seeking, or the lust for danger. These older folks have lived their lives quietly, never jazzed, always in tight control, paying their bills early, and never giving themselves over to hot sports, iced energy drinks, the rocky North Face, or marijuana and cocaine and promiscuous affairs on lazy afternoons. Suddenly urges of old appear and distort the view that man can change his base behaviors by will power and maturity.

Recent evidence reinforces the results for the drug agonists that stimulate hypersexuality and gambling and is now being widely debated in the treatment of Parkinson's disease. Additional observations indicate that drug agonists for dopamine also put patients on the path for excessive shopping, obsessive involvement in hobbies, and disruptions of sleep cycles.

Sensation seekers dig deep for the hormonal rush that brings satisfaction. He/she are slightly off center, aggressive, promiscuous, action-oriented, and into fast cars, horror movies, drugs, interactive video games, Twitter, Face Book, and rock and roll. The knowledge that they share is that it is all about getting high—the dopamine and testosterone kick that is crucial for defining life – a high that just can't last forever, they realize, and is as precious as the Hope Diamond.

Sensation seekers may often take excessive risks, but because of their narcissistic visions of success and low emotional attachments to others, they may have a lower than average rate of suicide. They may be killed in the frantic race to new summits, but they probably don't kill themselves, at least during their prime of life.

Here is a stunner. John J. Ray, a sociologist at the University of New South Wales, Australia, did a postal survey of Australians, sampling both their ideological stance and their level of experiential sensation seeking, and found that those individuals with a "radial-left disposition" are high sensation seekers. Moreover, radicals on the political left have a general need for novelty and stimulation, almost regardless of its source, and they use consumer products that they denigrate. It is almost as if they find novelty beautiful. Ray concludes: "High-minded ideals are often little more than a cloak for a need for excitement and change." Those who are hunting the thrills of hope and change may find a home in the political arms of chaos and near the steps of Wall Street.

Following up on the notions of John Ray, it would be informative to find that listening to the sing-song repetition of entreaties, demands, and promises delivered by extraordinary orators, such as those we heard during the GOP Presidential Primary, cause a sudden and electrifying surge of dopamine. As part of a homogeneous cohort, group consciousness might be shaped and solidified by the power of words and suggestions.

Marvin Zuckerman notes that several common risk-taking behaviors are correlated for both men and women in college. Risky driving, sex, drinking, drug taking, smoking, and gambling often occur together. It is not too surprising that drinking, smoking, drugs, and sex often occur together. These relations are not particularly strong, but many are statistically significant, and they do suggest that risk-taking behaviors and the associated highs are broadly expressed simultaneously, much like traits of psychopaths are joined.

I asked a friend what he thought about the legal action of senior citizens against drug companies because of the prescription drugs that set off a chain of compulsive gambling and hyper sexuality. He wondered why in the world they would sue a company for essentially making them younger and more vigorous, more involved in social interactions, and (probably) euphoric. He said that he worked hard to get these reactions and these guys are getting it free, so "What do they have to complain about?"

What I think it denotes is that psychopathic traits (and many other behaviors) are wired into just about everyone, but are only expressed to the extreme when they are triggered by the appropriate neural/physiological stimuli or relevant environmental cues. Behavior is in large measure a lock and key reaction. Specifically, these older folks possessed the biological engrams for youthful sex and taking chances, and the dopamine surge was the key that turned the locks. Such is life in the fast lane with the intermittent flow of dopamine and the strong feeling of perpetual life.

The Grand Prix: Mixing Fear of Dying and Commitment to Death

The undecipherable irony of sensation seeking is that the worshiper of risk-taking sometimes makes a pact with Lucifer for a euphoric life in exchange for exposure to an increased probability of death. Well, he/she signs no contract with the devil, and only infrequently refers to the commitment, but one can hardly avoid the alliance. Sensation seekers are drawn into the pact with every opportunity and every technological development. The invention of skis and the snowboard ushered in new levels of downhill sensation and risk. Similarly, the advent of the automobile and airplane brought us racing and sky diving. Rock climbing equipment increased the art of scaling rocks and climbing to mountain summits. New weapons and easy means of communication increased the ease of guerrilla warfare. Almost every advance in technology drew in sensation seekers that extended and overused technology for the dopamine high. It also saddled the participant with a closer relationship with death.

Coupled with the young male budge in many countries, sensation seeking increased over the years and was more and more directed toward conflict, revolution, and war. Death rates immediately escalated or remained high as the cultural potential. An early example of this association is evident with auto racing in the United States where 391 drivers died for the thrill of shaking hands with death.

Count von Trips, a flamboyant and famous German Grand Prix driver of the late 1950s and early 1960s, had a coat of arms that symbolizes the eternal sensation seeker: *In Morte Vita* (In Death there is Life). Death always stalks the sensation seeker, and often wins the tussle. As Sigmund Freud, the psychoanalyst postulated, death is often embraced as well as avoided (Eros and Thanatos, the wishes for life and the longing for death).

Competing against the American driver, Phil Hill, in the Grand Prix of Italy on a dreadful day, death took the life of von Trips. Trips committed a tiny error of no more than an inch and paid the ultimate price of living on the edge. Phil Hill was driving right behind Trips. Michael Cannell in his fast-action book, *The limit: Life and Death on the 1961 Grand Prix Circuit* (Hachette Book Group, 2011) gives us the moment of death for Count von Trips.

> *"…at 150 mph it was enough to sling him onto a grassy shoulder to the left. His wheels plowed the soft earth as the car rode up a five-foot slope where spectators stood two deep behind a chest-high chicken-wire fence. In an instant of explosive violence, the Ferrari slashed along the fence for about ten feet, shredding spectators like a big red razor, then bounced end-over-end back onto the track. The mauled car came to rest right side up with its wheels collapsed inward."*

THE GRAND PRIX CIRCUIT AND VISIONS OF DEATH

Five spectators standing along the fence died instantly, their skulls crushed by the spinning car. The survivors screamed, and the echoes returned the agony, in reaction to the death all around them. Bodies lay in scattered heaps. Ten more would die later. More than fifty were injured.

Hill zigzagged through the wreckage with studied care, never losing his patience, always with his eye on the prize.

Phil Hill, always measuring the odds and never recklessly challenging "the limit," won that race against his friend von Trips, becoming world champion. He at last walked away from the seduction of risk-taking and returned to his home in Santa Monica, where at the age of forty-four married Alma Baranowski. With a sudden loss of testosterone, I surmise, Hill lost his edge for danger and merged back into a traditional lifestyle.

Von trips never left his mind, however, as Hill measured his long life against the short and dramatic life of Trips. Deep nostalgia and regret eventually took him back to Pebble Beach with his wife, where he tried to relive his earliest triumph in a race for the Pebble Beach Cup fifty-eight years earlier. This may have been the same track that seduced James Dean and sent him forward to his death. Whatever Hill was looking for now escaped his reach.

At the end of his life Hill suffered from Parkinson's disease and other neurological degeneration. He was confined to a wheelchair and died in a Monterey hospital twelve days after his flight backward in time to Pebble Beach, finally giving in to his desperation at the age of eighty-one. He died August 28, 2008, paradoxically, the same day of the month, but in 1947, that the worshiped bull fighter Manuel Manolete was killed in Lincres, Spain, a bad day for the superstitious.

Both von Trips and Hill drove for Enzo Ferrari who in his earlier years was also a racer. Later Enzo's sensation seeking turned to designing and manufacturing a superior line of Ferrari race cars, several of which later became prized street automobiles desired by new generations of sensation seekers. I recently watched a video of the remarkable worship race-people have for Ferrari, as 360 almost all red racing Ferraris blew around a race track for the spectators.

Enzo specialized in speed and racing success, building mid-engine heavy racing machines that extended the "limit" to new levels of speed. The pistons of these cars are set at a low angle in order to lower the hood for better vision. Enzo was treated like a king, for decades making or breaking race drivers and spending millions of dollars on his passion. Enzo's extraverted and low empathy personality profile would have been perfect for a Shakespearian play. He wasn't happy with Hill's marriage, carping that occasional liaisons with women were fine for his team members, but marriage was a threat to speed (testosterone and dopamine are lowered as family responsibilities consume one's life). Strangely, Enzo never saw one of his cars race because he believed that each one was imbued with part of his soul and he refused to see it mistreated or ruined.

The thunder of motors and the thrill of speed remains present in our races, but the risk-taking has been reduced by benefits in technology and increased safety devices and strict regulations for car and driver performance and the protection of spectators. But the possibility is still in the mix as we recently watched Indy car driver Dan Wheldon die and burn at age 33 in a crash at a Las Vegas race (October 16, 2011). As cars piled up on the track Weldon's No. 77 car slammed into another car in front of him and he went airborne before crashing into a fence, briefly catching fire. Other cars were involved and some caught fire, but the drivers survived. At the hospital Wheldon was pronounced dead from "unsurvivable injuries." No spectators were hurt.

People who saw the crash said it looked like a movie scene in a Terminator movie, with fire, flying tires, and metal car fragments exploding through the air and into the pages of history.

Looking for the Final Answer

Why do so many racers and many of us take major risks where sudden death is a high statistical probability? During the early days of the Grand Prix the driver faced a thirty-three percent probability of being killed, yet thousands of drivers were willing to take the risk. Hundreds have died. In Cannell's book the ever-present fear of death was translated into a defiance of death and the hope for redemption. When the driver of a Formula 1 car was wedged into the cockpit of his car, in the late 1950s and early 1960s — no helmet or seatbelt, no top cover, with feet shoved through holes in the fuselage to manipulate the petals — the fear of death suddenly vanished for the existential fight and the mental calculation of speeding at 150 mph through the limit of steep curves. With the threat of death ahead, fear was forced into a deep pocket, a common happening with the sensation seeker and psychopath under siege. What the driver faced was the role of the dice and a path to immortality. One mile an hour too fast and he would spin out and the end would be sudden; one mile an hour too slow and the race is lost. At the start of the race the driver committed himself for the ride into hell and possible deliverance.

Rock climber Richard Gottlieb believes that his extreme risk-taking is a way of coping with death. "We open the door, see the Grim Reaper right there, but instead of just slamming the door, you push him back a few steps." Social psychologists interested in the basic urges of fear, creation, and conquering, understand the Faustian life and death bargains that tend to hold civilizations together before choices are lost. What can be a greater sensation than looking death in the eye? Spectacular things can happen.

Thanatos still haunts our activities. On August 7, 2010, the 35 year old long-time Swedish climber and skier Fredrik Ericsson fell to his death climbing the second highest peak in the world, K-2, a 28,250 foot peak in the Chinese-Pakistani border region. He and his partner were pushing for the summit when he fell to his death. It was his dream to ski from the summit all the way down to the base camp, a heroic attempt that no one has been able to do.

The usual question came up: Why would he temp fate when he didn't have to? One answer, voiced for Ericsson, said it clearly: "You think he'd prefer to have died in a car accident, or in a senior center? I think not."

The committed sensation seeker with low fear under stress is likely to succeed or speed to a fast death – an Evil Knievel kiss to the gods before he/she plunges toward immortality.

As I wondered about all of this, I settled on two points. The first is that great achievements cannot occur without risk, and death is often the co-pilot. The second is that when individuals square off against death they instinctively realize that sudden death is better than Parkinson's disease, long-term cancer, uselessness, wheelchairs and burning regret. There is only one life to use as you can. My guess is that Phil Hill would have wished to go like von Trips – a blazing torch of commitment, defiance, and longing for the end and perhaps a continuity of the soul.

Talk about a slip-up. On December 5, 2012 we witnessed an example of the cost of sensation seeking. Eight red Ferraris, one Lamborghini, and two Mercedes crashed in a horrendous pileup on a Japanese freeway. Speed was an issue. The police estimate that the large group of cars was traveling between 80 and 100mph when the crash occurred. The mass destruction of incomparable luxury cars was triggered when the driver of one of the Ferraris tried to change lanes to pass a Toyota Prius, hit the median barrier, and spun across the path of the other vehicles. A total of 14 cars were involved in the accident. Amazingly, no one was seriously hurt. The accident ruined at least one million dollars of fine engineering, according to police, but other estimates run as high as three million. Imagine all that luxury and engineering history gone in seconds. The police called the group of speeders "a gathering of narcissists." Heads will roll.

The Cultural Cause of Sensation Seeking

I can't resist a speculative moment. Earlier I said that increases in technology triggers higher intensities and more frequent involvement of he/she high-risk behaviors. Maybe the growl of a Ferrari engine, with its promise of victory and fame, drew von Trips and Phil Hill into their compulsive urges to press the limits of life. Perhaps that is the reason that von Trips and numerous spectators died on the track of the Italian Grand Prix, and was the reason that Hill backed down from more death-defying races in 1967. Who knows?

But the last 100 years of cultural advances may be responsible for the explosion of sensation seekers. This short period of time was the era of exciting changes and a growing sense that life was short, that there was no God, and that we all die. Nihilism is replacing optimism and confidence as a life force.

This was the era of Tin Pan Alley, prohibition and the mob, two world wars, Hitler, Stalin, Mao Tse-tung, and Roosevelt It was the time of the birth of the blues, jazz, and the explosion of science. Our cynicism of life and death was voiced by Pablo Picasso, William Faulkner, Ernest Hemmingway, Joseph Conrad, Sylvia Plath, and many other incredible thinkers. The cold philosophy of Darwin and Gregor Mendel held sway over our growing anxiety about death, followed by the shocking discovery by Watson and Crick of the indifferent DNA regulators of growth, senescence, and death.

We spiraled on, restless males and females increasing in numbers, losing our moral rudder, and asking how we should conduct our lives. For many,

THE GRAND PRIX CIRCUIT AND VISIONS OF DEATH

the answers came with technology, art, and an existential philosophy that left us detached from history, religion, moral restraint, and responsibility.

About the only avenues of expression left for surging populations of young males and females were risk-taking, drugs, sex, and a relief brought by the highs of dopamine and testosterone. Perhaps the "nothing" that we faced was transformed into the momentary pleasures of grand sensations, fast cars, bull fighting, mountain climbing, and jumping from high places.

"If that's all there is, then let's keep dancing," so sang Peggy Lee in 1969, giving us the new mantra of the sensation seeker and ultimately the surging numbers of psychopaths.

> "Ah, make the most of what we yet may spend, before we too into the dust descend."
>
> Omar Khayyam, Persian astronomer and poet

SOCIOLOGICAL PSYCHOPATHY

Even a purely moral act that has no hope of any immediate and visible political effect, can gradually and indirectly, over time, gain in political significance.

Vaclav Havel, Cezch playwright, president

The Collective Structure of the Human Mind

Individual psychopathic behavior often takes a backseat to collective psychopathy. Collective behavior, not necessarily restricted to undesirable people, can alter the human spirit and make us shiver in its presence. Group-think is not always individual-think, where freedom of thought can be submerged in group identity. Herd-like activity involves attitudes and beliefs that can be socially advantageous but may rarely be expressed by contemplative individuals. The atmosphere of the group may walk on a tightrope of emotion, inevitably merging with the crowd to temporarily or permanently override the individual personality and set the stage for new perspectives and actions.

Sociologists have known this for a long time, although it is left to us to use collective hypotheses to explain sociological psychopathy. Groups can be productive and enlightening, and they can also be destructive and dark and scary. *Collective consciousness* was a sociological term used by Emile Durkheim in 1893 to describe the shared beliefs and moral attitudes that operate as a unifying force within society. He did not have psychopaths in mind when he formulated the notion of collective consciousness.

Durkheim thought that the content of individual consciousness is largely learned and is held in common by members of their society. The outcome of group formation creates a mental and physical solidarity through mutual likeness, lending the group more power and effectiveness than with the individual components.

While short on evidence in the early days of sociology, most theoreticians probably accept these ideas as demonstrated. What the group theory lacked was a grounding in biology. There are innate behaviors that have evolved to ensure advantages of merging with others in common aims. Carl Jung, a famous psychoanalyst and a student of Sigmund Freud, brought us closer to understanding the biological forces that make group cohesion possible. He proposed that in addition to our individual and immediate consciousness, and independent of learned social behaviors, there is a second system of a *collective unconscious*, where the collective and universal archetypes of the mind reside. Today, the evolutionary psychologist would talk about social adaptations, instead of archetypes, that evolved for the understanding of the world and for effective group activities. Archetypes, I surmise, are the representations of universal forces, as with mental concepts of god, totems, and taboos.

In any case, Durkheim and Jung complement each other, as with two sides of a coin, leading us to the consideration of learned *and* genetic aspects of social behavior, collective consciousness being flexibly related to learned social values, collective unconsciousness providing the evolved substrate of universal perspectives.

Perhaps we should not push these "collective" analogies too far, and that's what they are at this point, but there may be one more that we should consider, as it now has currency and relates to religious ideals, morality, and visions of utopia. That concept is referred to as *collective salvation*, a Marxist precept that tells us that our economic and social struggles are progressive, and through class warfare, lead us to the perfection of man, and the birth of collective equality and social justice.

In our social development we have heard more than once that one's salvation depends on the salvation of everyone, suggesting that our perfection depends on the movement toward a classless society where equality and justice are found. The idea is sort of an "end of history" secular argument for the replacement of a god-religion with a unification of social principles.

Needless to say, these discussions require amplification for understanding and cannot be fully developed here. There are political implications that are related to the different points of view. They do, in total, give us the heuristic foundation for understanding the good and the bad, the altruistic and the psychopathic inclinations of group activities. There are also the practical implications of massive self-serving riots and continuing revolutions. At least we can explore the examples.

Fast and Furious

You might agree that some collective behaviors are not desirable. Some are thuggish and give us examples of social induction of psychopathic behavior. We still can relate to the herd images of these behaviors and marvel at their effectiveness.

A new version of group callousness and disregard for the rights of others is emerging across our nation, so novel and yet so frequent that it is tagged with a catchy title, *rob mob*. We can also call it group-inspired psychopathy. Like many other forms of collectivism it appears to be based not on fundamental needs, but rather on the opportunity for sensation seeking.

Generally, rob mob is the spontaneous banding together of teenagers for the purpose of robbing convenience stores and other places of business. It is akin to looting that we are all too familiar with. These rob mob groups are premeditative, setting them in contrast to opportunistic looting, yet the results are the same. These groups are put together using Face Book, texting on smart phones, or simply as contagious reactions within an existing group. At least one of these groups was formed during a bus ride by teenagers. In any case, the group forms, strikes quickly, pillages and steals, and then disperses, mostly without resistance or police action.

This incredible "grab and run" psychopathy is difficult to control because of its predatory quickness and rapid dispersal of the group. In one case in St. Paul, Minnesota, employees at the Holiday station on Wabasha Street called police about 9:40 at night indicating that they were being robbed. About 30 to 40 black youths entered the store, snatched dozens of juice bottles, candy, chips, and junk food, and nonchalantly departed. The police arrived minutes later, too late to make a difference.

No one was injured, yet two men were shot less than a mile away. The victims denied that they were party to the "snatch and run;" the shootings appeared to be gang related. The mob action was caught by a security camera.

Usually no one is hurt in these events, but there is at least one incident where a cashier was punched in the face. Violence is always a possibility. Young blacks, both male and female, currently dominate the mob robs, but other patterns of mob activities occur in all ethnic groups. Imagine what would happen if there were real food shortages?

No one knows why this disturbing behavior suddenly appeared in 2011. Certainly related to these acts of violence is a growing belief among the young, especially, in entitlement. These young people are mostly unemployed, yet they gain their subsistence from others who are employed and working for their benefit. "Occupy" groups come to mind as an example of entitlement attitudes. Not very thankful, I think. These are folks who are not hungry, and have most of the benefits of working stiffs. They literally stake out their claims, or burglarize businesses in plain sight with about 100 percent immunity from legal action, not very healthy in this society, and portending greater problems in the future.

Are they psychopathic? Well, they are narcissistic, have no empathy for others, and are criminal. Yes, by definition they are psychopathic.

Ideological Confrontations

More ideological, "occupy" protestors that started on Wall Street in New York, but have expanded rapidly, recently clashed with police in Oakland, California. Paint and rocks were thrown at police who were trying to disperse the group. A recent Fox News report indicates that the mob is attempting to occupy a vacant office building. The protestors also broke windows of nearby businesses. Police responded with tear gas and smoke grenades, and arrested about 100 individual group members.

The individuals respond like stereotypic juveniles – without a coherent philosophy and with an inability to articulate a plan. Expect more of these groups, driven by ideological puppeteers, and their own self-centered narcissism.

University PSU

The firing of coach Joe Paterno, age 84, by the Penn State University administration, for his failure to follow up on sexual assault accusations involving former Assistant Coach, Jerry Sandusky, led to a series of dramatic student demonstrations on campus and onto the downtown streets. Coach Paterno recently died, and the aggressive demonstrations have turned strangely somber.

At one point during the campus demonstration, President Graham Spanier spoke to the students who were staging a candle light vigil. Walking through the crowd the university officials were bid farewell by an eerie silence against the dramatic light of candles that highlighted the intensity of feelings in favor of coach Paterno.

But the Gandhi-ish protest didn't last and the demonstration in the city became bitter. Thousands of students tore through the streets of State College, PA, chanting the former coach's name, pushing over light posts, and overturning a television news van.

The students involved tried to justify their crude and senseless behaviors by opposing coach Paterno's firing, without regard to other points of view, university policies, or the facts. They were, and are, sensation seekers seemingly looking to reenact the student protests that are part of the dead past. Are they psychopathic? Not generally, but they had their momentary outbursts, none that were admirable. Many would agree that they should be in jail.

Football is King (Kong)

Far from just a "wave" sweeping over the crowd in the stadium, Oklahoma State University celebrated its rare football win over Oklahoma University December 4, 2011 by a thrilling and lop-sided 44-10 score. More than 58 thousand people pounded OSU on to its win. And, when the game was in its last few seconds, thousands dropped down (or were pushed) from an 8-foot stone wall and swarmed onto the field.

Jennifer Payne, a junior from Stillwater, was pushed over the wall by another female. The moving crowd was unstoppable. She later commented, "Luckily I didn't get injured, but I didn't have control of when I jumped off the wall. You just moved with the crowd."

The head of the "command medical post," Michael Authement, said, "Thousands of people stormed the field. You couldn't move, there were so many people." Thirteen were eventually treated for injuries, including eight who were treated at Stillwater Medical Center and with broken ankles. The exits were few and far apart, hindering the massive crowd in its attempt to escape the field. Luckily, there were no deaths.

The goal post went down in anguished victory, the blood-thirsty crowd finally satisfied. The psychopathology of the mob vanished with the growing concern of people to be done with it and get out safely.

Once again we encounter the demographic destiny of the young and restless that compounds the demons of hormonal abundance and intellectual deficit. Sensation seeking is the proximal cause of mob action and a subclinical expression of the common themes of psychopathy. For them, civilization is no obstacle to their narcissism, but when finally home again, civilization is of crystal importance.

The Unsettling Truth

We've seen mobs like those noted above over and over, thrashing through time, space, and property, acting on emotional cords and with the glazed-over eyes of the intellectually vacant. The difference today is that the riots against civility are almost daily happenings in the United States and abroad. Law and order and individual responsibility are coming apart.

Events, one way or another, are becoming political, with those who feel that they have special rights and with others who have scores to settle. There are many who are in the game simply because they get a cheap thrill. Mob gangsterhood is no longer widely sanctioned, and some is staged by third parties that have ideological agendas. Eventually everyone is hurt by explosive outbreaks of mobsters, sending a chill through our cities and telling us that empires are falling.

Mostly, our immediate defense against group psychopathy is to avoid areas and groups that foster herd behaviors. We needn't be caught in the matrix of protests; we can avoid criminalized neighborhoods; we can avoid large gatherings where emotions are running like rivers; and, we can still choose our friends and neighbors.

Long-term, we must not accept psychopathic behavior as the norm of a thriving society.

We can do our own protesting before school boards, in front of judges, and at the ballet box. And, we can turn back the fire of atheism for us or our neighbors and reverse the stone-cold Marxist philosophy, and teach our children by example and participation.

Increases in Food Prices and Psychopathic Riots

Of the several examples of group robs and riots, none can compare with what may be on the horizon for the United States and the world – food shortages. If and when food availability drops and/or food prices increase significantly, things will get serious, and riots will trigger food hunters and property wreckers. Rob mobs will escalate into massive looting, university protests will evolve into revolutionary movements, and sports mobs will inevitably cause widespread chaos.

Marco Lagi, Karla Z. Bertrand, and Yaneer Bar-Yam look through the glass darkly and see the compass needle point to desperate collective guerilla activities that will lead to massive killings and destruction of the world's assets (2011: arXiv.1108.2455v1 [physics.soc-ph]). Resting on their studies of North Africa and Middle East countries, they suggest persistent and increasing global social disruptions.

> "We identify a specific food price threshold above which protests become likely. These observations suggest that protests may reflect not only long-standing political failings of governments, but also the sudden desperate straits of vulnerable populations."

When I look at these data from the perspective of restless young males, of the 7 countries (including the Congo) where adequate information exists on the proportion of young males, all of the 7 were at risk for conflict behavior. The ratio of young males was far above average.

The paradox is that if food becomes scarce, as it is in sub-Sahara Africa and parts of Asia, the populations become debilitated and unable to protest or rise up against repressive and despotic governments. In Kinshasa province of the Democratic Republic of Congo, the people eat on the average only three days a week. Income is as low as $50 dollars per month per family. Families are forced to engage in "détestge," where the children and adults are forced to alternate days on which they eat some food – children eat one day and the adults eat on the next day.

The New York Times (January 1-3, 2012) said that it is nearly impossible for the starving population to rebel against a despotic government

> *"Protesters faced off with the police in Kinshasa after the deeply flawed presidential election in November. But the intense mass demonstrations many expected proved difficult to sustain, in part because of the daily struggle to survive."*

Rising food prices may initiate food riots, but if food is denied to the people by despotic governments seeking continuous control, the freedom to work, live, and prosper is denied. In the Congo the government is fixated on the extraction and sale of valuable minerals, such as copper and cobalt. All food production and distribution has been destroyed in the process, even in the fertile regions of the Congo. Other African and some Asian nations, as with Niger and Somalia, are on the cusp of famine and destruction.

Time is short and our burden is to help people prepare for that future, become self-sufficient, and, perhaps become farmers, and move away from the chaos and government repression.

Videos of Flash Mobs (www.mashable.com/2010)

Groups are not always irresponsible, thoughtless, or dangerous. Nor are all groups psychopathic – far from it. In fact, most groups follow sociologist Durkheim's concept of collective consciousness, where community values are widely shared and imbued into our psychic structure. These include families, schools, the devoted, sports enthusiasts, community groups, spontaneous groups to help others, musical and artistic demonstrations, and many of our public activities.

Inspiring representations of this altruistic and community spirit are the striking flash appearances of singers, dancers, and actors that initiate an artistic piece in crowded public places — eateries, sports venues, railroad lobbies, and other places where strangers congregate. The activities are planned to grow in steps until the audience is embraced and nearly all the strangers participate in the joy of common expression. It is a contagion of unification that is beautiful, beneficial, and reminds us that the spirit of he/she can never be confined. Check it out and enjoy the best of mankind's creative nature.

CAULDRON OF PSYCHOPATHIC SPIRIT

I have only ever made one prayer to God, a very short one: "Oh Lord, make my enemies ridiculous." And God granted it.

In the card game with the psychopath, you have to know when to hold and when to fold. If the game is stacked against you, it may be time to fold, cash out of the game, and go on down the road.

There is no Regal Road to understanding and acquiring immunity from danger, but knowledge is still the best defense, and experience helps. If there is a helpful generality it is this: there is a continuum of psychic deviation ranging from the common folks (you and me), to the sensation seeker, who is simply out there for the thrill, to the psychopath (aka sociopath) with crude strategies and criminal tendencies, and beyond to a reduced form of the psychopath, that of the Machiavellian, who is more flexible in motivations for winning.

The continuum from sensation seeker to Machiavellian is from indifference through thuggish behavior with complete lack of empathy, to competitive skills, intelligence and passions for success. Individual differences abound, but there remains a core of similarity that tips us off that there is a common origin and an overlap of personality traits.

Classical Machiavellian (Mach)

Machiavellianism is just short of an illness of the mind – a form of disturbed genius – centered on narcissism with Messianic visions, intertwined with traits of diminished sympathy, obsession with the perfectibility of man, condescension of the masses – sometimes charming, often callous – extraordinary capabilities for great deeds and penchants for surprising finishes.

Fashioned for risk-taking and focused on power and successes, the Machiavellian constantly flirts with historical accomplishments and imminent disaster. The historical record suggests that civilization would crumble to its center without the Machiavellian influence.

The literary origin of Machiavellian traits is Niccolo Machiavelli's dreary little book of 1514, titled *The Prince,* which illuminated selfish human behaviors that later were declared as Machiavellian. The case can be made that Machiavellian traits overlap with psychopathic behaviors, but the two forms of personality deserve separate categories.

Unlike the usual "street" psychopath, a Machiavellian is often highly intelligent, flexible in his strategies, with a deep appreciation of the arts, visions of human achievement, and constant hopes for a utopian future. This path is not always a panacea for social progress, but without the visionary fire of the Machiavellian, society would stagnate on the flat compromise of middle ground.

The Building Blocks for the Machiavellian and Psychopath

Not all of my encounters with Machiavellian individuals have been delightful. These people, usually male (three to one), share traits with common street psychopaths, but are unique in degrees of narcissism, intelligence, competitive skills, and passions for winning, They also have a sense of destiny, are generally low in affect and empathy, and high in sensation seeking, persistence, and grandiosity. They seem destined for success, but also lean toward lugubrious faces. In distinction to street psychopaths, Machiavellians often drive culture to higher levels of expression. They rarely end up in prison, almost never murder, and don't end up in the county morgue. Instead, within this heterogeneous group we find our greatest writers, artists, and intellectuals, scientists and educators, hard driving entrepreneurs, professional experts, and solipsistic politicians. Typically Machs (for short) dislike cooperation, rarely reciprocate with kindness, and avoid deep emotional relationships. If you lose your charm in their eyes, they are gone.

"Nate" is an obvious example. His strategy for success is immediate intimidation. When I first met him he wore a t-shirt that on the front read, "Choose your game, and practice, practice, practice." On the back it made his point, "And, I'll still beat you." In fact, he is a criminal lawyer who would aggressively defend a drug dealer, and in the end accept a generous bonus for services, yet refuse to join his client for dinner. The nuances of the case or the guilt of his clients matters much less than winning.

I consider the Mach as a psychopath with distinction, an enriched version of the common psychopath, but more intelligent, controlled, and productive. In fact, Machs can be good friends, if not threatened and if we don't care if they fail to return phone calls. We can accept their presence as we would a spectacular movie and still remain aloof and incredulous.

Another view of things is to believe that psychopathy and Machiavellians are cut from the same biological cloth. The major difference is that Machs simply have more mental dials, knobs, levers, and bells.

Machiavellians are of two voices, one of extreme self-centeredness, the other of dedication to personal and social betterment. Sometimes the dichotomy is sharp, but just as likely, the Machiavellian can comfortably slip from one personality profile to another. A colleague of mine, "Roger," detailed the dual sides of a Machiavellian female I call Temper. Here are his distinctions.

Machiavellian Traits	Non-Machiavellian Traits
Narcissistic	Intelligent
Charismatic	Charming
Hedonistic	Attractive
Risk-taker	Responsible
Dishonest	Friendly
Promiscuous	Problem solver
No guilt or remorse	Loyalty to old friends
Short-term sexual relations	Cooperative
Low anxiety	Altruistic
Self-destructive	Leader
Needs excitement	Organized
Grandiose	Generous
Drug user	Open about self
No fear	Vigorous
Selfish	Loves kids
Low empathy	Into music, science, sports

The lists make it sound as if we are talking about two individuals, but, no, it's the true variation within a single person. The good and bad may be about evenly balanced. The constant flux of the duality of personality traits of Temper is classic for a Machiavellian (Mach). Clearly these are unappreciated dimensions to Temper's complex personality, similar to other Machiavellians, which motivates me to tell the story. Roger told me that she did a lot of good for her friends and became a highly successful professional. That's a Mach for you.

Dr. Robert Hare, professor emeritus at the University of British Columbia, has spent decades studying psychopaths and has concluded that there are four factors that characterize their psychopathic-Machiavellian personalities: *Interpersonal, Affective, Lifestyle,* and *Antisocial*. These factors and their major traits are summarized below.

THE FOUR FACTORS	GENERAL PERSONALITY TYPE
1. Interpersonal Factor Glib, charming, callous, manipulative, pathological lying grandiose	Confident, gregarious, narcissistic
2. Affective Factor Lack of remorse or guilt, shallow affect, lack of empathy, irresponsible behavior	Emotionally stunted
3. Lifestyle Factor Sensation seeking, impulsive parasitic, lack of realistic goals	Risk-taking
4. Antisocial Factor Poor behavioral control, early behavioral problems, promiscuous, criminal versatility criminal recidivism	Lack of control

While not a perfect classification, the four factor theory can add to our confidence in spotting a psychopath or a Machiavellian. Regardless, in considering individuals, it is difficult to imagine the creation of scientific certainty, the assumption of military power, the demon-driven insights of literary genius, the political leadership of innovation, or the astounding achievements of the athlete without the unrestrained sensation seeking of the Machiavellian.

The Origin of the Psychopath May Have Been Where It All Started – Africa

The evolutionary birth place of the psychopath is not so different than yours or mine – as expected, DNA is mixed widely across individuals and generations, and traits spread themselves in different ways. The upshot of individual differences and multiple gene-traits is that some men and women accumulate more psychopathic traits than others, leaving an uneven wake of personality ingredients. Some individuals are loaded with psychopathic traits; others live in a psychopathic desert.

Statisticians have devised clever ways to describe the probability of events, the most ingenious of which is to plot events according to averages. Most distributions of metric events can be plotted in the form of a symmetrical normal distribution known as the bell curve. An example is IQ scores. The overall average in the population is 100, using current IQ tests, with 68 percent of individuals falling in the region of plus (+) or minus (-) of 34 points. Higher and lower IQs become less evident as we move in either direction from the overall average of 100. An IQ between 85 and 115 encompass the scores of the majority of individuals in the population. Scores of 150 or 50 are rare indeed, but they do occur.

Psychopathic characteristics typically distribute themselves in the form of a bell curve as illustrated below. Most extreme psychopaths form about one or two to fourteen percent of the distribution, the most extreme occurring at about two percent. These rare cases include the murderous combination of traits that we see among serial killers, hit men, sadistic killers, and genocidal maniacs that sometimes kill millions. The less extreme forms include what I have been calling the street (or common) psychopath, such as the recent "barefoot bandit" who is a general predator but never killed anyone, as far as we know, and the most frequent is the psychopath that I refer to as "high Mach," who is narcissistic, intelligent, but with low affect, followed by "low Mach," the least socially deviant of the psychopaths.

Distribution of Psychopathic Traits

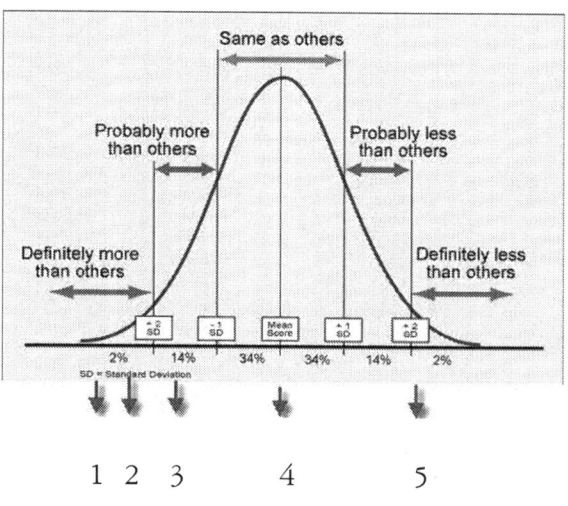

1 = Thuggish, genocidal
2 = High Machiavellian
3 = Low Machiavellian
4 = Male-like behavior
5 = Female-like behavior

The point is that the distribution of psychopathic traits, indeed most traits, will spread themselves out, with only some showing extreme deviancy. They occur as a consequence of averages selected by the force of evolution and showing individual variation and environmental modification around these averages.

In the minds of some, nothing more is required to explain psychopathy — it is an unusual statistical alliance among genes (DNA), natural selection, and individual differences of existing traits in a rather crude and expected manner.

We therefore expect that psychopathy is a natural occurrence of biological events — not without explanation, not an expression of insanity, and not a Faustian bargain with the Dark One, just variants on a distribution of possible events. The average is usually the most complex of the distribution, composed of a balanced condition of multiple influences. The extremes, on the other hand, are often related to fewer genes without balanced influences.

In this statistical view of the origin of psychopathy is a hidden implication, namely that the most extreme form, far out on the tail of the distribution, has the fewest genes underlying the condition and may be the most "primitive" and early form of *Homo sapiens*, oriented directly toward survival, fast sex, and great selfishness. Combined with other observations, it appears that more complex emotional and neural processes came later in humanoid evolution, such as empathy, guilt, and remorse, traits that require more elaborated orbital frontal brain functions. I hesitate to argue this strongly, but there is evolutionary logic here.

Said another way, the first successful male *Homo sapiens* may have been a lean mesomorphic (muscular) individual, with high testosterone, built for fast action, risk-taking, and even murderous inclinations, with a reduced higher level neural superstructure. Refinement, additions, and complex social mechanisms, including monogamy, were of more recent phylogenetic genesis.

The argument is sound, but frankly we lack verifying details. The more primitive and early form of human, exemplified by the male psychopath, may have been the nucleus from which the more social forms of human arose. Would it bother you if your ancient ancestor on the African savanna were an unrefined creep peeking around the bushes?

The Psychopath Lives Fast and Doesn't Give a Damn

Short-term strategies of the psychopath and the long-term strategies of the non-psychopath contrast in degree but not quality. Both are encouraged by natural selection for gene reproduction, and each provides lessons in living.

It appears that psychopaths are actually more successful at getting sex than non-psychopaths. Peter Jonason from New Mexico State University in Las Cruces, New Mexico, tested 200 college students for three common psychopathic traits – the "dark triad" of psychopathy, including narcissism, thrill-seeking, and deceitfulness, and asked the students about their attitudes in sexual relations and about their sex lives, including the number of partners they had and whether they were seeking brief affairs.

The short of the study was that those males who scored higher on the dark triad of personality traits tended to have more sexual partners and a desire for short-term relations. At least today, and possibly in our evolutionary history, psychopathic traits of manipulation, narcissism, and sensation seeking have a reproductive advantage over the males with non-psychopathic tendencies. This is exactly what we would suspect, namely that psychopaths are short-term rapid maters with less interest in love and long-term relations. It doesn't mean that non-psychopaths are not successful at sexual relations, but that they have a set of reproductive traits that enable them to prosper with longer relations, especially those that require secure bonding and concern for offspring.

A balance of traits within each mating strategy, psychopathic and non-psychopathic, is necessary for two successful reproductive strategies, accounting for the high intracorrelations among traits within strategies. The success of the psychopath not only depends on charm and manipulation, but also requires high levels of intimidation and aggression. Similarly, the success of the non-psychopath requires commitment to the female and her orientation toward resource acquisition for the survival and growth of offspring.

The two modes of male reproduction (short-term or long-term bonding) are distinctive but each requires a mosaic of correlated traits, suggesting that natural selection not only works on specific traits, but also on clusters of interrelated and cross-supporting functions. The short-term male mating strategy of the psychopath rejects any and all trait qualities that would tie him to the mating situation, such as empathy, love, guilt, remorse, true confession, competitive aggression, responsibility, and interest in children. He remains aloof and individualistic on every issue. Non-psychopaths, who strive for long-term mating relations, emphasize traits that the psychopath rejects. That type of male goes for romantic love, commitment, low testosterone, low aggression and non-abusive behaviors that would damage his relations with his partner. He has a communal attitude and sensitivity to all human processes. Not surprisingly, traits within each strategy are highly correlated; everyone has to be consistent with the others or the harmony is lost, and so are the mating opportunities with the female. The table offers plenty for the reader to contemplate.

Contemplating The Differences in The Short-Term Mating Strategy of The Psychopath and The Long-Term Strategy of The Non-Psychopath

Trait	Short-term Mating: Psychopathic: Individually Motivated	Long-term Mating: Non-Psychopathic: Socially & Communally Motivated
Polygamous	Yes	No
Promiscuous	Yes	No
Fast sex	Yes	No
Mate Commitment	No	Yes
Love	No	Yes
Self-gratification	Yes	Yes
Charming/glib	Yes	No
Testosterone	High	Low
Aggression	Yes	No
Intimidation	Yes	No
Manipulation	Yes	No

Lying/deceitful	Yes	No
Jealousy	Yes	Yes
Risk-taking	Yes	No
Self-confident/cool	Yes	No
Fearless	Yes	No
Murder	Possible	No
Frontal lobe dysfunction	Possible	No
Responsibility	Low	High
Energy Level	High	Low
Criminal	Possible	No
Abusive	Possible	No
Information strategy	*System 1	System 2
Alcoholic/drug use	Probable	No
Reduced fear/anxiety	Yes	No
Empathy for others	No	Yes
Narcissistic/ messianic	Yes	No
Guilt/remorse	No	Yes

System 1 refers to the neurological complex related to quick and decisive action; System 2 refers to more complex information processing involving a heavy involvement of cortical processes.

We make a *faux pas* when we think that some men are exclusively psychopathic while others escape that stain — they all are guilty when we narrow the differences, that is, when we compare ordinary men to full-blown psychopaths and compare unexceptional men to women. Most men, if not all men, have at least some characteristics like the garden variety of psychopaths, but thankfully, to a lesser degree. And they differ from most women by 180 degrees. Maybe it is true as John Gray wrote: *Men are from Mars; Women are from Venus.*

Forty-one traits or motivations of adult men are listed in the table below. The traits were deliberately chosen that show typical "masculine" traits that are often found in normal adult males. The 41 entries were clustered into seven arbitrary factors. If nothing else, the data suggest how "normal" males compare to known psychopaths on a number of traits. The entries obviously do not reflect the conditions of all males, and are merely illustrative of trends in the direction of psychopathic behaviors.

Major Traits and Objectives of Typical Men
The Seven Factor Theory of Normal Behavior

Factor	Name of Factor	Male Orientation
1	Biological	High testosterone, developmental quirks, more disease, surplus in population, shorter life span.
2	Physical	Muscular, active, energetic, loves sports, fine cars, high risk activities.
3	Mental	Shallow affect, little interest in arts, forgetful, belief in his intelligence.
4	Competition	Buddies/gangs, quick to anger, aggressive, career-minded, enjoys fights/dangers, dominance-oriented, enjoys business, politics.
5.	Reproduction	Quick mating, polygamous, little child care, adultery, no deeply family oriented inclinations, guards female; is individually oriented.
6.	Behavioral	Interest in hunting/guns, alcohol/drugs, maybe single, innovative.
7	Psychological	Narcissistic, irresponsible, gambler, lies more than females, little guilt or remorse, high ego, little sympathy for others.

Relative to women or adolescents, adult males tend to be more muscular, energetic, and higher risk takers, compete more for positions on social and business ladders, tend to have higher blood testosterone, show more developmental errors and disease, are emotionally shallow, tend toward short-term mating relations with little child care, have a sports and hunter mind, like guns, are more innovative, and are liars, gamblers, have large egos, show little sympathy toward others, and are irresponsible and narcissistic – *more than women and adolescents, and less so than the typical psychopath.*

The similarities between the male down the street and what we normally classify as psychopathic are unmistakable. Their wives, girlfriends, and female colleagues are often poles apart from the male on most traits.

Five conclusions follow.

1. Male psychopaths are nothing special in terms of qualitative trait profiles; they match up closely with the evolved traits of all males.

2. Males differ mainly in degree of trait expression, not quality of expression.

3. The thin line between male psychopaths and the "general" male suggests that the typical male is just a short distance from becoming a "true" psychopath, and indeed may cross that line under some circumstances.

4. Given these similarities it is unlikely that the wide range of psychopaths has unique neurophysiological mechanisms underlying their behaviors. We should not necessarily find brain damage that will explain male deviations, except in the most extreme cases.

5. Finally, the fact that men and women are vastly different speaks volumes about critical reproductive strategies and how they are managed. It seems at times that we are looking at different species. Female evolution, ever since internal fertilization first occurred, has been along a different highway.

The telling differences between the non-psychopathic male and his psychopathic counterpart is that the married guy down the street may engage in bad behavior on Friday night, but on Saturday he is feeling guilt, shame, and remorse, and on Sunday there are flowers on the kitchen table for his spouse or girlfriend, and he may be in church seeking redemption. The true psychopath, taking risks on Friday night is exaggerating his feats on Saturday to his buddies and on Sunday he may rest and plan for an eventful week. Guilt, shame, and remorse are in his vocabulary but not in his heart.

Dealing with the Complexity of What We Want

We've gone a long way in a short time. My only defense is that it is important to connect the evolutionary origins of psychopathy with the natural selection for adaptive traits that define our species, and also come to understand the "normal" characteristics of male and female behavior along with the critical variations that separate the normal individual from the extreme sensation seeker, the Machiavellian personality, and the true psychopath.

The conclusion that we must live with is to realize that the science of behavior is at the frontier of knowledge. No "principle" of behavior is carved in stone and we are far from completing our investigations. But there may be a Final Theory of Behavior somewhere on the horizon, one that stands on the foundation of behavioral measurements, neurophysiological investigations, and evolutionary scrutiny of our origins. We have the broad outline of what we are after and can therefore go forward with confidence and excitement.

From basic knowledge comes not only a greater understanding of normal and deviant behaviors, but also allows us to offer the troubled and dangerous individual alternatives for a better future. It also gives the rest of us the visuals for identifying the many faces of psychopathy.

PSYCHOPATH THEATER

> Name me, if you can, a better feeling than the one you get when you've half a bottle of Chivas in the bag with a gram of coke up your nose and a teenage lovely pulling off her tube top in the next seat over while you're doing a hundred miles an hour in a suburban side street
>
> P.J. O'ROURKE, U.S. JOURNALIST:
> "HOW TO DRIVE FAST ON DRUGS WHILE
> GETTING YOUR WING WANG SQUEEZED
> AND NOT SPILL YOUR DRINK" (1987)

The house lights dim, the curtain opens, and out jumps a psychopath wearing nothing but a mask of sanity. You've been had!

The disguise is necessary – a wall of safety between you and the truth. Peppering you with visions of seduction, the psychopath hides the sinister motives of manipulation and the hollow shell of caring. The play is on.

He/she dares not reveal his true self. Thus, there are only two choices in his mind, building a stage play that charms and disarms – captivating you during Act I before fleecing or bedding you in Act II, or if discovered too soon, drawing up a new resume and becoming someone else in Act III.

The hard-core psychopath is generally not interested in actual work or contributions to a cause; he/she would rather build a beguiling fantasy, lie when necessary, and blame others as well as overpowering situations for poor performance.

Lying with great sincerity keeps the story flowing, protects the actor's illusions, and covers his or her poor performance. The psychopathic lies add to the story line and open the doors of manipulation and conquest. No wonder the psychopath makes a great (but short-term) lover and friend and a terrible boss and co-worker. No wonder that the psychopath blames everyone in sight for his or her failings.

The Professional View

The major difficulty, as I see it, is to definitively mark the psychopath. We don't want to make a mistake here, as not all bad behavior is psychopathic and captivating charm may at times be sincere.

But what does it mean when I describe a street mob as psychopathic? No, it doesn't imply that all individuals of a mob are psychopathic. When judged individually and away from the herd, individuals may come across as rational and meritorious. Nor does my judgment of the mob imply that individuals described as psychopathic are identical in personality profile or behavior.

Some psychopaths are driven by basic needs — for food, sex, and shelter. But others, often with substantial intelligence, seek power, fame, money, and control. The former are hard-core psychopaths; the latter are Machiavellians. Two individuals may be equally psychopathic on some metric of scale, but act out their perspectives in incomparable ways. A friend of mine, "Russell," and a highly valued professor at a major university gives us the startling array of contrasting traits.

Meet a Tough Mach with Two Special Traits, Intelligence and Style

A few years ago a friend and former graduate student of mine visited my ranch in Texas. He and I have been friends for over 40 years, but we rarely see each other and mostly talk on the phone or communicate by email. I'll refer to him as Russell. He is a professor at a well-known university. He told me that he was working on packaging a series of DVD lectures for distribution and wanted my suggestions on his teaching style. Sharing a couple of drinks he gave me a demo lecture which was astonishing.

He positioned himself loosely, gave me his best smile, and began as if directing a Beethoven symphony. With a polyphony of arm and hand movements, all synchronized with his gruff and dramatic flair, he told me in a sonorous voice about terrorists he met on the Gaza Strip, how they lived, and what they feared, first pianissimo, then allegro, moving to a staccato emphasis for rhythm, then a surprising crescendo, and, with time, a diminuendo and a fall of arm movements that draws his audience together for the climax. I was taken by his orchestration — all as if he had created the harmonic whole from the bottom up, nothing missing and nothing too exaggerated. As his hands drew to a stop he saw me watching for the first time, smiled as if coming out of a trance, and asked me what I thought.

It dawned on me that he had mastered his black belt in judo and later in karate, and he lectured within the framework of katas that were so much a part of his life — fluid and musical as good katas are. Katas are fighting movements, timed for effect, almost like chants. They are hypnotic to both the actor and spectator, and are the basic movements of defense and destruction. The effect coupled with his lecture was stunning. He had taught this way for years, telling large student audiences about aggression, explosive violence, men and women with great courage, and CIA mystery and intrigue. I am told by his students and faculty that his charisma has students taking his classes for the second or even third time.

Is the show part of his basic personality, or can anyone do it? No, anyone cannot; it takes a break from the drab world of reality in which many of us live and an extraordinary obsession with one's self. His unconscious and natural movements of body, particularly his hands and fingers, choreograph the theatre of his mind, compelling rapt attention by those in his sphere, a great argument for the benefits of narcissism.

His students have aged since he first kicked off the show, leaving Russell's close friends as state and national politicians, contractors, teachers, bankers, restaurateurs, and musicians, who still call him for advice. There is no end to what charisma can do, especially when it is stained ever so slightly with psychopathy.

The best and revelatory story he once told me was when he drove a female student home after conducting a late seminar. As Russell exited freeway 96 on the way to the student's home and stopped at a red light, a black Chrysler screeched up to his passenger side. The driver of that car looked down at Russell's little Miata, top down, and yelled over the girl's head at Russell: "Hey man, got any money?" Russell boomed back, "Yeah, I've got more money than you'll ever have." The stranger hesitated, recovered, and said, "Okay, give me some." To that Russell reached to his side, pulled out a 9mm automatic revolver, looked up at the big Chrysler, and fired seven shots into the guy's door, knowing that the bullets would never make it through the massive door. The guy peeled out in a cloud of smoke.

The whole episode went down in seconds — a Mach attack that probably saved him and his student. Russell grabbed a flashlight and looked around in and outside the Miata, making sure he found the seven shell casings, in case he had left his finger prints on them when he earlier had loaded them into his revolver.

A week later (I guess after the student recovered from shock) Russell was filling his gas tank at a local Exxon station and that same guy wheeled up, recognized Russell and bellowed, "You son-of-a-bitch, look what you did to my car," jumping out and pointing to the holes in the door. Russell hung the gas hose up, and as steady as a slab of granite, looked squarely at the guy, and said, "Next time I'll aim higher." That ended the conversation and the guy drove off without another word. I don't know if Russell's story is true, exaggerated, or partly imagined, but I've never seen my friend flinch at possible physical encounters and as far as I know, he's fearless.

Sometimes I recall Russell at a small cocktail party I hosted years ago for a few faculty and students. Circulating through the group I overheard a heated conversation going on between Russell and a faculty wife. She remarked to Russell that most policemen were sensation seeking psychopaths and bullies, and they should be removed from law enforcement. With a straight shot to the heart of the discussion Russell said, "Think about this. In the middle of the night the lone cop in a cruiser gets a call from headquarters to investigate a warehouse break in. The burglar was thought to be armed and dangerous. Backup would be moments behind.

"The cop finds the warehouse, dives through a broken window, flashlight in his left hand, a 38 special in his right hand. It's black and scary in there, but his adrenalin kicks in and he's excited. Okay, tell me, who else would go in there but a sensation seeking psychopathic bully? Do you really want a nice mild guy with a family at home, several college degrees, and a deep-seated fear working for you to clear the human debris, or do you want the guy who is willing to jump in and do the job that might end his life?"

It was one of those clarifying moments. He's intelligent, talented, and looking for a worthy challenge. He'll find it too, and I sure as hell don't want to be caught in the middle.

Those who live in a mix of equal amounts of anxiety, guilt, and shame, have a difficult time understanding Russell. Why doesn't he express guilt and remorse for his startling behaviors? Well, why should he? He honestly doesn't feel these emotions strongly, and who are we to say if the absence of guilt and empathy is always a bad thing? Ask a Mach if he feels guilt and if he doesn't lie about it, he might tell you that he hasn't the slightest idea what the hell you are talking about. What we must also ponder is why we think it's so important to live with the emotional trinity of anxiety, guilt, and shame. In the opinion of successful Machs these emotions that we believe elevate our lives and are emblematic of our humanity, drag us down and do not necessarily make us a better person to face the challenge in the environment. "Chairman of the Board," Frank Sinatra exhibited a clear hint of his Mach attitude when he commented, "Show me a guy who has feelings and I'll show you a sucker."

Making judgments more difficult for the student of psychopathy, the individuals may specialize in psychopathic displays, as with promiscuity, aggressive intimidation, story-telling, or pitting allies against opponents.

If our paintbrush is applied too broadly, all individuals seem psychopathic. We may be marking all adaptive traits from evolution past as selfish and devious. On the other hand, and equally questionable, if a small paintbrush is used for detail, all individuals seem to require a distinctive nomenclature.

Take criminality as our example. If criminal behavior is viewed as psychopathic (using broad brush strokes) any and all criminals are psychopathic. But if a criminal must also have a stunted emotional bearing (detail painting), then only some criminals are psychopathic.

Add another crucial trait, say; lack of empathy, or excessive narcissism, even fewer criminals will be branded as psychopathic.

Thus, depending on the traits that we insist as indicative of psychopathy, we expand or contract our definition and increase or decrease its frequency. There has been a trend toward the latter strategies, in hopes of eliminating "false positives," until we now recognize only about one percent of the population as psychopathic.

This cannot be true, as we see the syndrome so frequently in so many contexts and intensities. More accurately, the frequency of psychopathy is around 15 percent. There has to be a reckoning between the small and large paintbrush approaches, between the estimates of one and 100 percent.

Another prism that suggests a relatively high frequency of psychopaths in our population is one that focuses on the environmental factors that push psychopathy to higher levels, as with demographic features of the young males' restlessness, situational factors that stimulate testosterone and dopamine secretion and add to the fire of psychopathic behavior, early experiences and developmental co-factors that modify behavioral expression, and mob activities that suddenly drive psychopathic behaviors to street violence, or the crunching of goal posts after an exciting and successful football game.

The definitional problems will never be solved to everyone's liking. To some extent, it must be admitted, diagnosing psychopathy is art as much as science. Justice Potter Stewart gave us the lead in 1964 when he was asked to define "hardcore pornography." His view fits my own perspective when it is applied to psychopathy.

> *"I shall not today attempt further to define the kinds of material I understand to be embraced within that shorthand description {"hard-core pornography"}; and perhaps I could never succeed in intelligibly doing so. But* **I know it when I see it,** *and the motion picture involved in this case is not that." {Emphasis added}*
> JUSTICE POTTER STEWART, CONCURRING OPINION IN
> *JACOBELLIS VS. OHIO* 378 U.S. 184 (1964),
> REGARDING POSSIBLE OBSCENITY IN *THE LOVERS.*

We continue to probe for clear definitions of psychopathy, but before that is possible, we can say clearly: "I know it when I see it."

The Science of Art

Robert Hare has found a partial solution to our quest for a scientific standard in describing the major features that drive the psychopath, and puzzle us. Through a long process of testing prison inmates, as well as other populations, Hare concludes that 20 traits, distributed across four primary classes of personality (Factors), characterize most psychopaths and distinguish them from most non-psychopaths. The Psychopathic Checklist is shown below.

Psychopathic Checklist*
(After R.D Hare, 1990)

Score Trait as 0, 1, or 2

Person Trait	Doesn't Apply (0) Applies Somewhat (1) Definitely Applies(2)
Glib/charming	
Needs stimulation	
Pathological lying	
Manipulative	
No remorse/guilt	
Shallow affect	
No empathy/callous	
Parasitic lifestyle	
Poor behavioral control	
Sexually promiscuous	
Early behavioral problems	
Lack of long-term goals	
Impulsive	
Irresponsible	
No responsibility for self	
Many short-term relations	
Juvenile delinquency	
Recidivism	
Criminal behavior	

*Checklist is generally applicable to males, females and juveniles

Scoring Outcome:

0-25 Non-psychopathic
26-30 Mild psychopathic
31-40 Psychopathic

Reference: Hare, R.D. (1990), The Hare Psychopathy Checklist Revised Manual Toronto: Multi-Health Systems

The reader can revisit the distillation of traits into the four factors that often characterize psychopaths (discussed earlier). The four factors are *Interpersonal Factor* (emphasizing narcissism), *Affective Factor* (emphasizing emotional characteristics), *Lifestyle Factor* (risk-taking), and *Antisocial Factor* (degree of personal control).

The total score for the Hare Checklist is important, but so are the types of personality traits. An individual who is glib, charming, and narcissistic may be wildly different than an individual who lacks empathy and is irresponsible, but both may be considered psychopathic, depending on their total test scores.

The point of special interest to us is that the distribution of social traits among psychopaths may be different, and yet in overall personalities, they may all be rationally described as psychopathic. And yes, mobs may be psychopathic in their aggregate, even if they form one day and disperse the next.

Complexity Increases

The new version of the Diagnostic and Statistical Manual of Mental Disorders (DSM-V), the Bible of the psychiatric profession, attempts to unravel the complexity of psychopathic behavior. In this new manual narcissism and psychopathy will no longer be described as a trait separate from Antisocial Behaviors, a decision that illustrates the variety of forms that narcissism takes. The recommended description of Antisocial Behaviors is expected to take the form given below.

Antisocial/Psychopathic Type
(Recommended Revisions for DSM-V)

Individuals who match this personality disorder type are arrogant and self-centered, and feel privileged and entitled. They have a grandiose, exaggerated sense of self-importance and they are primarily motivated by self-serving goals. They seek power over others and will manipulate, exploit, deceive, con, or otherwise take advantage of others in order to inflict harm or to achieve their goals. They are callous and have little empathy for others' needs or feelings unless they coincide with their own. They show disregard for the rights, property, or safety of others and experience little or no remorse or guilt if they cause any harm or injury to others. They may act aggressively or sadistically toward others in pursuit of their personal agendas and appear to derive pleasure or satisfaction from humiliating, demeaning, dominating, or hurting others. They also have the capacity for superficial charm and ingratiation when it suits their purposes. They profess and demonstrate minimal investment in conventional moral principles and they tend to disavow responsibility for their actions and to blame others for their own failures and shortcomings.

Individuals with this personality type are temperamentally aggressive and have a high threshold for pleasurable excitement. They engage in reckless sensation seeking behaviors, tend to act impulsively without fear or regard for consequences, and feel immune or invulnerable to adverse outcomes of their actions. Their emotional expression is mostly limited to irritability, anger, and hostility; acknowledgement and articulation of other emotions, such as love or anxiety are rare. They have little insight into their motivations and are unable to consider alternative interpretations or their experiences.

Individuals with this disorder often engage in unlawful and criminal behavior and may abuse alcohol and drugs. Extremely pathological types may also commit acts of physical violence in order to intimidate, dominate, and control others. They may be generally unreliable or irresponsible about work obligations or financial commitments and often have problems with authority figures.

Source: The American Psychiatric Association, 2010

This stunning description clearly incorporates the wide sweep and consequences of malignant self-love and other psychological traits common to psychopaths. One wonders when the final curtain comes down, where the threshold is between charm or clever oration and manipulation and deceptions.

Valid Distinctions Come to Us in Literary Form

Quantification of traits and psychological studies represent common approaches to the understanding of psychopathy, but they are not the only approach. Even poetry may reveal the line between psychopathy and non-psychopathy. The hormonal and behavioral spectrums between sensation seekers and non-sensation seekers are in opposition as are their philosophies. We can also see the split in poetic terms, such as with Lord Byron spitting fire and invectives and Robert Frost giving sage advice through words of flowers and flowing streams. Neither understands his brother; neither cares a whit about the other.

And Thou Art Dead, as Young and Fair Lord Byron Selected Stanzas

> And thou art dead, as young and fair
> As aught of mortal birth;
> And form so soft, and charms so rare,
> Too soon return's to Earth!
> Though Earth receiv'd them in her bed,
> And o'er the spot the crowd may tread
> In carelessness or mirth,
> There is an eye which could not brook
>
> I know not if I could have borne
> To see thy beauties fade;
> The night that follow'd such a morn
> Had worn a deeper shade;
> Thy day without a cloud hath pass'd,

And thou wert lovely to the last,
Extinguish'd not decay'd;
As stars that shoot along the sky
Shine brightest as they fall from high.

A Prayer in Spring Robert Frost

OH, give us pleasure in the flowers today;
And give us not to think so far away
As the uncertain harvest; keep us here
All simply in the springing of the year.

For this is love and nothing else is love,
To which it is reserved for God above
To sanctify to what far ends he will,
But which it only needs that we fulfill.

Reading Byron and Frost is like listening to a sensationist and a landscape artist. William Hazlitt, a friend of Byron, said this about him:

Whatever he does, he must do in a
more decided and daring manner than
any one else; he lounges with
extravagance, and yawns so as to
alarm the reader.

Robert Frost said this about himself:

And were an epitaph to be my story
I'd have a short one ready for my own.
I would have written of me on my stone:
I had a lover's quarrel with the world.

There it is, two irreconcilable halves of a whole: the beast and the beauty, moving within the deep layers of the unconscious or the deliberations of the frontal lobes. Here is a philosophical note for you to think about.

Slip-Ups and The Dangerous Mind

There seems to be an invisible line dividing people in their preferences and allegiances — organic and inorganic forms falling on one side of the line or the other. For example, the playful mind reaches out for jagged lines, squiggles, unusual people, spicy foods, loud music, new experiences, strange animals, beauty, new sex, and poets like Lord Byron. Another more introspective mind attracts traditional geometric figures, straight people, common foods, familiar places and animals, soft music and the poet Robert Frost.

Mysteriously and truly remarkable, for one person jagged lines, spicy foods, loud music, new experiences, and Byron have a common essence — to some extent they are interchangeable or at least intertwined. For another with a different brain, closed and predictable lines and figures, straight people, traditional pets, common foods, and Robert Frost are fundamentally equal and interchangeable. On one side of the invisible line is the sensation seeker and the psychopath, and on the other side is the conservative and traditionalist, and rarely the line is crossed. It is either Byron, who walks the narrow beam of destiny, or Frost, who embraces the benevolence of nature.

From the constellation of related needs and strategies comes the single essence of the mind, either a risk-taker or a nester. While informative to scientists, it doesn't take a psychopathic checklist or a sensation seeking scale to understand if you are on one dimension of psychological processes or on an entirely different dimension. One clue is perhaps enough to tell. Are you on Byron's side or Frost's. Raise the curtain and find out.

TROUBLE AT HOME AND IN THE OFFICE

A friend in power is a friend lost.

Hensy B. Adams
U.S. Historian

Power is not only what you have
but what the enemy thinks you have
SAUL ALINSKY
U.S. RADICAL ACTIVIST

I love power. But it is as an artist that I love.
I love it as a musician loves his violin, to draw out
its sounds and chords and harmonies.
NAPOLEON BONAPARTE
FRENCH GENERAL

> It is difficult to find a reputable American historian
> who will acknowledge the crude fact that a
> Franklin Roosevelt, say, wanted to be feared.
> To learn this simple fact one must wade through
> a sea of evasions: history as a motive force,
> when, finally, power is an end to itself, and
> the instinctive urge to prevail the most important
> single human trait, the necessary force without
> which no city was built, no city destroyed.
>
> GORE VIDAL, U.S. NOVELIST

How Does the Psychopath and the Non-Psychopath View Each Other?

John Milton saw the light in *Paradise Lost* when he said, "His tongue dropped manna, and could make the worse appear the better reason."

The accumulation of power often changes a person from an outgoing, considerate, and agreeable individual to an arrogant and self-centered ogre. Science writer Jonah Lehrer, penning for the *Wall Street Journal* (August 14-15, 2010), points to a survey of organizations that found "The vast majority of rude and inappropriate behaviors, such as the shouting of profanities, come from the offices of those with the most authority."

Surely, the sudden surge of a malodorous leader – over and over, without regard to form of business, geographical variation, and cultural origin – opens a door into the deep and universal archetypes of human struggles for power and grand designs for reproductive success. Why does it happen so often. Perhaps as Henry Kissinger said, "Power is the greatest aphrodisiac there is." Additional reproductive opportunities, not to mention other goodies, may be the bottom lines.

After all, evolution is a competitive game, giving rise to behaviors for survival and reproductive advantage, pure and simple. Individuals who can quickly "get the lay of the land," can then assume power over the environment, and dictate strategies for others to follow. They can more readily get sex, gain wealth and prestige, and acquire followers to help with the chores.

People give authority to those that they genuinely like – those with emotional appeal – only to see their Machiavellian side bloom with the power that he/she inherits. Dacher Keltner, a psychologist at the University of California at Berkeley, compares the acquisition of power to neurological patients with brain damage to the orbito-frontal lobes – like Phineas Gage who had a steel rod blown through the frontal area of his brain as a result of a construction accident. The event changed him immediately from a considerate friend and employee to a raving madman.

Power is not necessarily evil, but it can be. Power can focus a person's attention on essentials, and benefit the organization he/she serves, but a leader may also distort information and often finds it difficult to make complex decisions. With a spike in power a leader can lose empathy for those without power, manipulate others, resort to lies, and operate defensively. In power, the initial benevolence can quickly disappear and the reign becomes defensive, heavy-handed and sometimes merciless. But, rather than analogizing the rise to power as malignant, like a disease, we can better understand it as nature's way of building successful psychopaths who might benefit from the accouterments of power.

Living a Phony Life Triggers Phony Behavior

We are well aware of the notion that "You are what you eat." The oldest reference to this idea may come from the Roman Catholics' belief that the bread and wine of the Eucharist are transformed into the body and blood of Jesus (Transubstantantiation).

> *We offer and present unto thee, O Lord, our selves, our souls and bodies, to be a reasonable, holy, and living sacrifice unto three; humbly beseeching thee that we, and all others who shall be partakers of this Holy Communion, may worthily receive the most precious Body and Blood of thy Son Jesus Christ, be filled with thy grace and heavenly benediction, and made one body with him, that he may dwell in us, and we in him.*
> THOMAS CRANMER
> ARCHBISHOP, 1549

People are sometimes overcome with the hunger for blood and flesh, striving to realize in symbol or reality the nature of the sacrifice. Why do serial killers often resort to cannibalism? What deep unconscious motivations cause this behavior?

Physical and mental transformation by social pressures extend to a related idea, namely, that "You become what you do." That belief goes back historically at least to the philosopher and scientist, Aristotle (384-322 BCE).

> We become just by performing just actions,
> temperate by performing temperate actions,
> brave by performing brave actions.
> ARISTOTLE

> Watch your thoughts, for they become words.
> Watch your words, for they become actions.
> Watch your actions, for they become habits.
> Watch your habits, for they become character.
> Watch your character, for it becomes your destiny.
> ANONYMOUS

We see the equivalent transmutation when a person suddenly assumes power and immediately begins to act as many other powerful people act, with lack of empathy, callousness, arrogance, narcissism, and ruthlessness. It is as if the assumption of power extends their behaviors into the domain of psychopathy.

A related metamorphosis occurs when a person assumes the characteristics of a phony, or at least how they believe phony people to be. Wray Herbert, writing for *Scientific American Mind* (September/October, 2010) gives examples of abrupt changes in personality among women who dress up in expensive and sophisticated clothing. Three scientists, Francesca Gino of the University of North Carolina, Michael I. Norton of Harvard Business School, and Dan Ariely of Duke University explored the pitfalls of fake adornment.

A large experimental group of women were given Chloe sunglasses to wear. The glasses were genuine, but half of the women believed that they were wearing knockoffs. The researchers were interested in knowing if wearing counterfeit sunglasses – a form of dishonesty and self-deception – could affect cheating behavior and attitudes toward others.

What they found in tests of honesty was that fully 70 percent cheated during the tests for honesty when they thought that they were wearing knockoff glasses. In contrast, only 30 percent of those who thought that they wore authentic Chloes cheated. Those women who believed that they were wearing fake Chloes saw other people as less truthful, more dishonest, and more likely to cheat in business dealings. They saw other people as they saw themselves.

The investigators, publishing in the May 2010, issue of *Psychological Science,* concluded that "Faking it makes us feel like phonies and cheaters on the inside, and this alienated, counterfeit "self" leads to cheating and cynicism in the real world."

These examples of transmutation show how easily psychopathic traits arise from blood, power, and greed. The genetic influences, independent of the environment, demonstrate a basic biological influence on psychopathy. In addition, the instances of personality change associated with transitory irrational beliefs or by modeling of others warns us not to overstate the genetic impulses on behavior. Not only do individuals give new birth to themselves, but mobs, nations, and civilizations act to direct personality expression.

In addition, we can see that psychopathic characteristics (socially unapproved behaviors) are not automatically evil or even undesirable. On the contrary, those characteristics that sometimes lead to greatness – narcissism, confidence, charisma, feelings of manifest destiny, risk-taking, focused intelligence, arrogance, manipulation, seeking of stimulation, innovation, and paranoia – are tied to psychopathy. Without them civilization would strangle.

In effect, power leads to Mach tendencies of quick action, narcissism, loss of cognitive control, and diminution of empathy. It is as if the need to operate within an arena of power can sometimes provoke the deeper survival traits of aggression, loss of affect, self-serving behaviors, and impulsive reactions to threats. Given more power, individuals may also revert to short-term mating strategies with several partners. People infected with power circle the wagons, look for enemies, and attack.

The Mach tendencies are modules of the human personality, usually shielded from recognition by the indifference of the public, but expressed more earnestly because of challenges of the environment and the assumption of power. It is not a long walk from charity and trust to selfishness and paranoia – the seeds of psychopathy germinating into new forms like a tadpole morphing into a frog. It is amazing how easily a change in circumstances can almost immediately transform individuals into stereotypic leaders, or cynical followers. The changes in personality expression may be only temporary, but even so, they are significant changes and can roll the dice in unexpected directions.

While "blood lines" and evolved adaptations set the base level of psychopathic expression, there is obviously a great deal of flexibility in how and when these traits are manifested. The core traits of humans might be tightly woven into the DNA of history, and not easily changed, but the wide sweep of the environment, including hormonal levels, attitudes, ideologies, degree of competition from others, feelings of destiny, male age ratios, availability of mates, cultural pressures, and rewards and punishments for good and evil, can tip the expression of psychopathy at the blink of an eye. In simplistic terms, we must always consider psychopathy as the interaction between evolved imperatives, genes, neurophysiology, culture, and developmental processes.

Psychopaths Lack a Sense of History

Indeed, there is a lot of variability in the expression of psychopathic traits, but there is a small percentage of the population whose behaviors are relatively stable under a variety of circumstances and unlikely to change when faced with pressures of the environment. It is as if some individuals are mute to negative and positive reinforcements. This quality is beyond the usual flexibility of human reactions, and is more determined than that of the Machiavellian personality, where psychopathy is less of a determining feature. Unlike the earlier examples, the inheritance of power does not suddenly change the personality; rather, the personality is oriented in that direction from an early age. It may be disguised in the work place and in daily interactions, but the inclination wafts across the spectrum of fortunes.

This characteristic is a strangeness of hard-core psychopaths that seems impervious to the flow of information around them; they cannot easily adjust to novel ideas and changes in the environment. Even as the psychopath ages, the incidence of psychopathic acts decreases, but not, apparently, the motivations underlying such acts. Testosterone may waft away, but we remember the challenges of earlier days. It is the other side of the biological coin where psychopathic traits come and go depending on opportunity and demand. Neurophysiologists are especially interested in these stable traits because in their research they act as the neural baseline, those girders that shore up more common variations. Historians and philosophers have a role to play, as the data suggest that hard-core psychopaths and those that embrace those same traits, lack a sense of history, a damning quality in a world short on predictive capabilities.

Niall Ferguson, a Harvard historian, explains in his prophetic book, *Civilization: The West and the Rest* (The Penguin Press, 2011), that in order to understand the past, we must learn to step into the shoes of those who went before us. We must sympathize [or empathize] with their shorter lives, where they lived, and how they dealt with uncertainties, often under harsh circumstances.

Insights about history not only occur as a result of our present economic and social environment, but because we are able to sense what people faced in the past and their implications for understanding the present.

Ferguson leads us back to the great Scottish economist Adam Smith for the origin of this idea.

> *"As we have no immediate experience of what other men feel, we can form no idea of the manner in which they are affected, but by conceiving what we ourselves should feel in the like situation. Though our brother is on the rack, as long as we ourselves are at our ease, our senses will never inform us of what he suffers. They never did, and never can, carry us beyond our own person, and it is by the imagination only that we can form any conception of what are his sensations. Neither can that faculty help us to this any other way, than by representing to us what would be our own, if we were in his case. It is the impressions of our own senses only, not those of his, which our imaginations copy the imagination, we place ourselves in his situation."*

History, according to this view, has no credibility if it is not based on our sympathy for those who died before us. There has to be an emotional bonding or history is stale and lacks human motivations.

Adam Smith's admonition to probe the past with sympathy unintentionally gives us a better module for understanding the hard-core psychopath, or his pretender, who displays a minimum of empathy. He/she, without an emotional attachment to the past, is entirely a person without a past, without a history, and therefore, without an ability to use history to predict the future. "History is bunk," said Henry Ford, not in tune with those of the past. In full he said this:

> *"History is more or less bunk. It's tradition. We don't want tradition. We want to live in the present and the only history that is worth a tinker's dam is the history we made today."*
> HENRY FORD, U.S. INDUSTRIALIST, INTERVIEW
> FOR THE CHICAGO TRIBUNE, MAY 25, 1916

He also said that anyone can have the color of his choice for the Model T Ford as long as it's black.

The psychopath is said not to have a conscious, but, according to Adam Smith's view, a more accurate appraisal would be to say that he/she has no history. Lacking empathy, there is no way he/she can grasp the significance of the past in making decisions. He/she may be able to visualize a historical chronology, but the sense of why people responded as they did does not register the import of the events. Instead, what the psychopath carries in his head is a fixation on the present and a lusting for instant gratification. The lifeline to his history, and his ability to grasp the significance of peoples' lives, has been severed by his emotional privation. Even the short history of his parental beginnings will probably lack substance. His future, too, has reduced significance because he cannot accurately identify with others' view of the world. In short, he/she, like an electronic robot, is stuck with the gyrations of the present – always the present, never the past, unable to touch the future – the present, the present, the present.

IDENTIFYING THE PSYCHOPATH

When you have eliminated the impossible whatever remains must be the truth.

Sir Arthur Conon Doyle
Sherlock Holmes

Dr. Robert Hare describes the sinister profile of the psychopath using 20 rudimentary traits grouped under four factors (see an earlier discussion). As a rough and ready checklist, it pinpoints the major variations that, in their extreme, define the psychopath. The development of the psychopathic checklist was a major advance over more intuitive measures. It gave us a specific composite of traits, a breakdown of traits into clusters of related traits, and quantification of a major personality complex. It remains the gold standard of the academic investigator, the forensic psychologist, and the neural physiologist who would like to relate these major traits to other behaviors and specific areas and tracts of the brain.

The checklist does not, however, provide an entry into the flexibility of the psychopathic personality and the nuances of its expression. The presentation of the checklist is too formalized and restricted to give us an adequate picture of the swirling nature of the individual, and it can't be used by the majority of people to determine the depth of psychopathic involvement. It doesn't allow for "street identification" of the psychopath under daily conditions. The checklist may give us a generic picture of the major traits used to determine psychopathy, but in its efficiency in a laboratory setting, it also limits the very probes we need to unravel a personality and add to our everyday protection. Psychopathic profiles come in many flavors and forms, and we need something that we can apply "on the fly" to reach our conclusions.

Our problem is one of triangulation; we need the more subtle discriminators that reveal the edgy characteristics that together define the psychopath. It is one thing to define the psychopath as emotionally blunted (Factor 2), but quite another to find that a person is fearless, unresponsive to loud noises, and uncomfortable to be around. We are looking for a broad set of criteria that will allow us to specify the range of psychopathic traits under everyday conditions.

In short, we need a new and more varied map of psychopathy, an amalgam of traits that is based on lifestyle habits and gives us practical information about the conduct of a person and our expectations as to what individuals may do under certain conditions. We present our criteria here, realizing that these too are incomplete and restrictive and require refinement.

Most of the "signature" traits we use to define the presence and degree of psychopathy are not by themselves definitive measures of psychopathy. But they are pathfinders. They are correlated with the psychopathic personality, but individually are not sufficient to allow us to reach a conclusion. Many of these when considered together do, however, give us a lucid and enriched view of a person's motivations. The use of many criteria of potential problem traits, almost like alchemy, gives us insights that we might otherwise miss. We will learn whether or not to trust a person or expand an association.

Signature or pathfinder traits include the following. Many problematical traits you can detect simply by talking to an individual and asking questions, although some may require more research. To our chagrin, the psychopaths and Machiavellians who thrive on action and loquacious manipulation rarely leave a written record of their crises and achievements. It would be helpful to have a written record of their behaviors and motivations. Patience and experience are two important Sherlock Holmes attributes to keep in mind. One should also consider how easy it is to be taken in by a psychopath looking for a victim. You can be overwhelmed by his or her charm and manners and trust him without verification. Frankly, the more independent you are in your thinking and actions, the less likely that you can be manipulated by Mr. Bad. If you are "of your own mind" you don't need his sticky solicitations, his passionate lies, his crummy investments, or his imperialistic and obnoxious manners.

Lifestyle Trait Clusters

Unusual dress (e.g. all black clothing), unkempt, tattoos, tacky, a verbal line that seems too good to be true, often humorous, sarcastic, or ironic, loud and obnoxious. Too much self-confidence, constant use of "I" pronoun, grandiose ambitions, frequent offers of help, rebel without a cause.

Interests in extreme sports (skydiving, rock climbing, snowboarding etc.), stimulating drugs, gambling, alcohol, smoking, rock and roll, body building, martial arts, fast cars, motorcycles, risky investments (e.g. day trading), avoidance of family activities, surprising openness. Mesomorphic (muscular) body type, presumably with high levels of testosterone and dopamine.

Aggressive moves (for display and shock), talk about confrontations or extraordinary accomplishments, obsessive interest in guns or other weapons. Unexpected gestures and quick (flash) smiles that seem out of place or insincere.

Reduced fear, looks right through you, steady under stress, rigidity of thought and motivations, no response to unexpected stimulus changes (such as a sudden clatter of dropped dishes), doesn't sweat, uncomfortable to be around.

Need for party atmosphere, need for fast profits, inability to keep a job or retain long-term residence, no interest in traditional education, difficulties at work, disliked by subordinates, few friends. Little interest in local or national politics.

Too much confidence, offers unusually profitable opportunities, blames others for faults, pokes fun at others, too prominent on social media websites (e.g., Face Book).

At work: intimidates others, inability to please, no consideration of input from colleagues or subordinates, insincere, impatient, lies about his work history, or is inconsistent about his work background. As an authority figure, demands much of his subordinates. Most of his energy is applied toward deception and very little toward accomplishment.

Disinterest in history. Cognitive difficulties, emphasis on emotional reactions, possible dyslexia, history of conduct disorders, early abuse of animals. Relies on fast reactions in an emotional and mostly aggressive manner.

Narcissist, feelings of personal destiny, ingratiating attitudes, constant lies and contradictions. Looks down the nose at others.

Uninterested in family matters, no concern or interest in children or long-term relations. Lack of interest in community affairs and local politics.

Crowding these many characteristics into a short list of potential problem traits, here is my summary.

Individual Traits

Pushy, especially when sex is involved.
Lack of empathy for others, callousness and disregard for others.
Repetitive broken engagements or lateness for appointments.
Glibness of manner, grandiose, self-centered.
Lying and presenting contradictions.
Blaming others.
Aggressive, explosive, violent outbursts.
Story-telling, high-spirited orations.
Easily bored, looks for thrills, often funny.
Peripatetic, agitated, manic-depressive, compulsive.
Stories too good to be true. Charming.
High praise for future victims.
Concentration on quick gratification.

Social Traits

>Promiscuous.
>Few long-term friends.
>Not interested in long-term relations.
>Petty criminal behavior.
>Dogmatic social ideas.
>Superficially gregarious.
>Feelings of superiority.
>Cult participation.
>Looking down the long nose (condescension).
>Aloof and secretive with little explanation of background.
>Mimic others' behavior (leaning from cues).
>Failure to complete even simple tasks.
>History is bunk attitude.

If you feel that you may be swindled or taken in by sweet talk and false promises, don't hesitate to be suspicious. It takes time to make presumptive decisions, but with practice and time they come easier. If you're planning to buy a product or a service from a possible predator, insist on getting references, and then follow them up. If you apply for a job and the boss is immediately critical or indifferent, consider other opportunities. Ask direct questions of company officers and employees. Don't jump into a situation that may turn out badly and waste your valuable time.

Do a Google search on the name of the individual that concerns you. It may not reveal much, but it's worth the try. Try the name of the individual in the local phone book, on Facebook, LinkedIn, and Twitter. You may discover interesting fascists of the person's thinking. Run a check on the person's criminal background (such as with: www.Govpolicerecords.org). This is a free service. Ask the person for his or her address and phone number, usual requirements on a background check. Find out who his or her friends and relatives are and check around. Check the phone book of any city or county the person says he/she is from. You might be surprised at what lies beneath the smooth surface of a pirate. If the person has something to hide, and can't stand the heat of your inquiries, he/she may simply vanish at this point.

An acquaintance of mine had a habit of referring to his exploits in Vietnam as a "special forces guy." He claimed several military medals and commendations, but when I asked to see his medals and commendation, he told me that a burglar broke into his house and stole them. I followed up on this unusual response by consulting a website devoted to exposing false military exploits (Wannabe Heroes: www.homeofheros.com/valor)/ I couldn't find anything that indicated he had even served in the military special forces, let alone winning a silver star with clusters, as he claimed. This same man was later accused of swindling a woman out of half of her inheritance by getting her sick husband to will his property to him.

The Big Lie

Psychopaths know who they are, but often lead multiple lives as they split their personalities to fit the moment. The 1960's movie *The Great Imposter* starring Tony Curtis was a stunning biography of Ferdinand Demara who spent his adult life living the shadowy existence of false identities.

Demara joined the army in 1941 and in quick succession borrowed a buddy's name, Anthony Ignolia, faked his own suicide, assumed another name, Robert French, and blossomed into a "religious psychologist" sans degree. His false identities were discovered while he served in the military and he went to prison for eighteen months.

A committed psychopath, his imprisonment did not change his risk-filled life, and his resume took on large proportions. He successfully passed himself off as a civil engineer, an assistant prison warden, a sheriff's deputy, an industrial psychologist, hospital orderly, a lawyer, a Benedictine and then a Trappist monk, a literary editor, a teacher, and a cancer researcher. One teaching job led him to prison for another six months.

His most famous caper was that of masquerading as surgeon Joseph Cyr on a Canadian Navy destroyer HMCS Cayuga during the Korean Conflict. He actually performed surgeries and dispensed medicines while on shipboard.

Demara was indeed the great imposter. We will meet others as bold and multi-sided, lying so effectively and frequently that they virtually have no stable identity. They transform themselves quickly and live the lies of the moment, often avoiding detection for long periods and doing great damage. The small lies used to gain your confidence are often a prelude to a spectacular and costly proposal or theft.

The records of hundreds of others like Demara tip the balance in favor of the hypothesis that psychopathic dissemblers represent a natural variation of the human theme. Their presence runs from the common street variety to commanding leaders that influence much of what we do. They also suggest that pathological lying, typical of the psychopath and the Machiavellian, is the basis for identity change — once the pattern of lying becomes a natural part of one's lifestyle, so effective that even the liar believes his or her lies, it's a small step toward assuming an entirely different personality. Little lies can lead to the big lie, from a teacher to a surgeon, from a bus driver to an airline pilot, or from a benefactor to a bully.

The Forever Search for Virtuous Behavior

Ecclesiastical interests always move toward the control of unruly behavior. One of the early spectacular attempts to instill a sense of morality in the restless brain was also perhaps the most successful. It occurred at the moment when Moses spoke with God at the top of Mount Sinai and returned to the people with the Ten Commandments of the Lord engraved on stone tablets.

These sectarian images fueled the expansion of the expression of Western economic and social dominance. They were also intended to squelch the psychopaths among us, even though that personality type was yet to be described. If I were to ask you to quickly indicate which commandment provokes your interest or concern, which one would you choose? Quickly now.

The Ten Commandments

1. Thou shalt have no other gods before me.
2. Thou shalt not make unto thee any graven image.
3. Thou shalt not take the name of the Lord thy God in vain.
4. Remember the Sabbath day, to keep it holy.
5. Honor thy father and thy mother.
6. Thou shalt not kill.
7. Thou shalt not commit adultery.
8. Thou shalt not steal.
9. Thou shalt not bear false witness against thy neighbor.
10. Thou shalt not covet thy neighbor's wife.

Opening my envelope with my predictions, you would find numbers 6, 7, or 10, and possibly 5, as most significant in your thinking. All of these could have major influences on your reproductive fitness. Numbers 1 through 4 would not quickly come to mind, as they are not immediately part of our biological concerns, and 8 and 9 are situational in most of our lives. How did I do?

Thoughts about sins and virtues became more pointed and less spiritual over the centuries. The "Seven Deadly Sins" are the most interesting, as they resist religious dictates and appeal to our hedonistic motivations and our searching for freedom of expression. We do spend time dealing with what I call the "Seven Deadly Virtues," but I submit that the "Seven Deadly Sins, the "Seven Biological Determinants" that shape our lives, and "The Seven Psychopathic Behaviors," often corner the market of the mind. I make the comparisons among these traits in the table below.

Seven Deadly Sins	Seven Deadly Virtues	Seven Biological Determinants	Seven Psychopathic Traits
Lust	Chastity	Excessive sex	Promiscuity
Gluttony	Temperance	Over-indulgence	Will to power
Greed	Charity	Avarice	Material pursuits
Sloth	Diligence	Lack of ambition	Aloofness
Wrath	Patience	Rage	Destructive urge
Envy	Kindness	Insatiable desire	Blaming others
Pride	Humanity	Boasting	Narcissism

The ecclesiastical and secular prognosticators of moral and immoral behaviors give us another view of the psychopathic strategy, again as part of the structure of the human evolutionary tree, and the normal behaviors that are sometimes expressed to the extreme.

Indeed, the broad structure of our western civilization – those attributes that we consider virtuous, and thus are in contrast to the psychopathic image – can be used as a cultural template against which we measure the psychopathic mind.

Ask yourself, when considering the collective consciousness of society, how well individuals fit the non-psychopathic model. I am not suggesting that the conceived moral template is desired or not, but only that it provides a traditional and accepted backdrop against which you can more easily identify a psychopath. If an individual is greatly at odds with the following Western Canon, one might consider the individual as a candidate for the Big P (that is, psychopathy).

Community Consciousness: The Western Canon

1. Community identification

Interest in local political activities.
Involvement in religious functions; goes to church.
Volunteer activities; charitable donations.
Interest in local school activities, sports functions, broad community activities.

2. Job commitment

Regularly employed or self-employed.
Long-term job history and involvement in current job.
Interest in personal success and in bettering oneself.
Supervisory responsibilities.
Interest in starting business.

3. Expectation of cultural conformity

Reliability in meeting expectations.
Goal directed inclinations.
Discipline and specificity of focus.
Reciprocal relations (reciprocal altruism).
Interest in non-aggressive conflict resolution.
Orientation toward community projects and community health.

4. Attitudes toward marriage and Infant Care

Concern with stable marriage.
Concern with marital fidelity.
Interest in having children and infant care.
Interest in family stability and financial status.
Interest in child education and advancement.

Many of these attitudes and cultural expectations may sound superficial to some of you, but consider this. In several regards the collective consciousness is not simply arbitrary features of civilization. They embody the formula for success at the biological level, unveiling the universal attitudes associated with social cohesion and ultimately genetic success. Thus the Western Canon developed around the fundamental attributes of humans, as individuals strove for community identity and stability of important relations – the collective unconsciousness on the job – all of this is more in conformity with non-psychopathic strategies. Thus the Western Canon shows us, inadvertently, what traits are important for achieving genetic success. The esteemed social thread also helps us identify and protect ourselves and our loved ones from the contrasting psychopathic social chaos.

As Sherlock Holmes remarked at the start of this chapter, "When you have eliminated the impossible, whatever remains must be the truth."

Detecting Lies and Contraditions

The advantages of lying can be immense and may determine human and other animal success. Human lying confers dividends in much the same way that other animals use displays, coloration, movements and gestures, and specific vocalizations to add or detract from animal qualities.

Lying is an especially important tool, as it allows a person to bypass a problem, blame others for failures, cover a crime, mislead or dissemble, defend against attack, exaggerate a quality, construct a story, conceal intents, bear false witness, add exciting variations to a story, acquire sexual partners, and reap a number of social advantages. With fast talk with plenty of charm, gold chains, new suits, Rolex watches, fast cars, hanging out in the "right" places and with the "in" crowd, people make statements of dubious validity and defend them as true.

Everyone lies occasionally. We lie in order to manipulate a situation, enhance our resume, hide a fault, or protect a loved one. People often deny lying, or may justify a lie. "White lies" don't seem to count against us, and omissions are par for the course. Chances are that if someone you know tells you that he/she never fibs, you can bet with high certainty that he/she just lied. Strangely, he/she may not realize that he lied.

Deliberate lies are often times pricy. Changes of perjury are possible and lies may evoke charges of fraud. Friends are lost, and marriages flounder on life's common lies. Trust can be lost in a moment, partnerships buckle. Contradictions poison an atmosphere and repeated lying can escalate into threats, violence, and even wars. No one is immune from the consequences of lying.

As you can therefore imagine, people defend against the charge of lying, even when their frequency of telling whoppers is low and of little consequence. There is nothing strange about rebuttals, denials, and the cover-up of lies, because one's reputation is worthy of defense.

In the extension of time, lying is a contingent strategy for success, applied carefully for effect. It is also a recurring evolutionary battle between the liar and the seeker of truth, or between one liar and another. The battle may be pursued below one's sense of awareness, accounting for the face of denial and our opposition to unpleasant accusations or disturbing facts. The best falsehood is one in which the perpetrator passionately believes to be true, perhaps more prominent among psychopaths than non-psychopaths. It is better that we don't recognize or exaggerate our own lies, for the future depends on our reputation.

The Depth of the Psychopathic Lie

Lying is the hallmark of the psychopath. My larger point is that lying is a hard-wired strategy for survival and reproduction. The psychopath often hones dishonesty with gusto as he/she pursues his goals without guilt or remorse. We hardly recognize our own lies, not to mention those of the psychopath whose entire structure is stitched together with lies. He/she is more likely to consider himself an artist, rather than a fraud.

The psychopath is so adept at lying that a lie disarms us when it should alarm us; it flatters us when we should be repelled; it compels us when we most need our discriminatory judgment. Unfortunately, the lies are often delivered with authority and with the charm of a viper, when we most need to be defensive. Even when we suspect that we are being lied to, the significance of those lies hardly fazes our opinion. "Oh, but he/she is so charming." "He/she means well, after all." "And he/she is funny." "Who cares if he/she lies now and then; doesn't everyone?" "Regardless, he/she is so much fun to be with."

Charm trumps lies. But the real difficulty and important moment is when an admirer of a psychopath admits his or her folly and finally tells the story for what it has become, and not for what one wants the story to be.

How to Catch a Lier

Recent work suggests more clearly the dysfunctional traces of psychopathy in the written and spoken words. The psychopathic existence depends on the effective use of lying – lying about one's past, deceiving others about the absence of empathy, and doing what is necessary to construct believable stories to cover malicious intents. It is the pathological lying – continuous and captivating – that can expose the machinations of the psychopath.

There are many myths about lie detection, ranging from beliefs that no one can beat the polygraph, to believing that particular eye movements and emotional motor reactions can usually reveal the liar. Studying the scientific literature, what little there is, does not encourage the viewpoint that we can become expert at detecting liars. Some individuals are better at lie detection than others, and practice in looking for lies helps, but there are no perfect rules for lie detection. On the other side, some psychopaths are better liars than others, and there too, practice is important. It boils down to a "battle of the minds," deception vs. revelation, cover-up vs. exposure, winning vs. losing – a game that is on at all times.

The ultimate answer for the lie detector is to observe the subject continuously, with sensitivity to the frequency of probable lies, and the inconsistency of replies. Both habits – lying and contradicting – become apparent over time. It is not so much what the lies are about, but how often it occurs and how often one can see contradictions. If you understand the pattern of psychopathic lying, the specific content of the message is unimportant.

For example, if someone is tells you the merits of a car he/she is trying to sell you, but in unclear about the characteristics of the car and evasive about its origins and the deed of sale, you probably should not buy the car, regardless of its low price. In another instance, I overheard a conversation between a man and woman where deflection of information was involved. The man was trying to convince the woman to go to bed with him. He was charming and gave compelling reasons for her to give in. She finally said that she would consider it if he would produce a medical certificate that he was free of sexual disease. He immediately launched into a defense of his personal hygiene and talked about his virtues, but he declined to talk about a medical exam. Eventually, without a word she picked up her cell phone and walked away.

As Marshall McLuhan, a linguistic scholar once said, the medium is the message. How the message is delivered or not delivered is often more important than the content of the message. Look for the medium and don't concentrate on the message

Lying is Embedded in the Language that We Use

A mere 13 years has have given us considerable information about distinctive speech patterns among psychopaths. Chad Brindley and his colleagues (May,1999, *Personality and Individual Differences*) documented that psychopathic speech among male prison inmates is poorly integrated, compared to that of non-psychopathic speech. There are exciting linguistic techniques being developed that are specifically directed at unveiling duplicity and deceit by psychopaths. Some of these can be easily applied "in the field." No detailed testing is required and the process of uncovering lying (the medium) is not lengthy. There will always be "false positives" in these strategies, but they can increase the probability that lies will be detected.

The cautionary note is that your detection of lying will not be foolproof, but you can do better than chance. Even the experts at detecting duplicity rarely bat 300. We cannot expect to see "the big lie," that will reveal the machinations of the psychopath, but we can lay out some parameters so that we can better reach decisions.

Several different types of lies are expected. Unfortunately, the psychopath uses them all and there is nothing specifically a part of his or her repertoire. But, as the psychopath continues to lie adroitly, we can begin to see the major patterns. With experience our batting average will increase.

Many small lies may provide as much information as one big lie. You are likely to see these forms of lying.

1. **Fabrication**: a scenario often used to complete a story. If the subject tells you that he was at thecomputer store, he/she can quickly fill in untrue details to explain why he was there.

2. **Bold-faced lie**: an obvious lie. If he/she explains that he was late to meet you because his mother was in an accident, but then brushes it off as not important, he/she is probably lying.

3. **Lying by omission**: he/she tells part of the truth, but leaves out important details. He/she may say that he stopped at the bank on the way over, which may be true, but he might have been there attempting to cash a bad check. Or, infidelity is almost always side-stepped until a "visual" happens.

4. **White lie**: a lie that has no major consequence, but is still untrue. It is often used to divert attention or to protect revealing another motivation. Politicians are particularly adept at this form of lying.

5. **Noble lie**: a lie that can cause discord if discovered used to cover an act that can cause dissention or threaten someone's power or prestige.

6. **Emergency lie**: a self-protection lie to prevent retaliation for another action, such as indicating that he/she didn't recognize the robber for fear of reprisal.

7. **Lying under oath:** Perjury.

8. **Exaggeration:** Overemphasizing the truth.

9. **Sarcasm or teasing:** often used to jest or divert attention from more important issues.

10. **Contextual lies**: taking written or verbal statements out of context to isolate and put forward a particular point of view.

11. **Promotional lies**: putting forward a product or service or oneself in an exaggerated way in order to get someone to buy or use the product or service.

There may be universal signs of lying, only some of which have established validity. These include eye movements and changes in pupillary dilation or contraction, body language, gestures, and small emotional reactions, stiffness of movement, perspiring, curtness, changes in cadence of speech, attempts to distract, overemphasizing one's innocence, repeating what the observer is saying, aggressive reactions to questioning, overdetailing for emphasis, contradictions, use of third person, the frequent us of unusual words, and blaming others or particular situations. As researchers Klaver, Lee, and Hart found (*Law and Human Behavior,* 2007, vol 31, 337), psychopathic lying among male prisoners include a wide number of correlated traits. Here is a brief summary of their study.

"The current study examined psychopathy and nonverbal indicators of deception in an incarcerated sample. Nonverbal behaviors were coded from videotapes of 45 offenders telling true and fabricated stories about crimes. Interpersonal features of psychopathy were associated with inflated views of lying ability, verbosity, and increases in blinking, illustrator use [gestures ?], and speech hesitation. While lying, the more psychopathic offenders spoke faster and demonstrated increases in blinking and head movements. Indicators of deception in offenders were somewhat different from those typically observed in non-offender populations. These findings indicate that personality factors may have an impact on nonverbal indicators of deception in criminal justice settings where the detection of deception is of utmost concern."

The Fragile Truth **

No system of investigation is free of bias and the polygraph does not always lead to the truth. Often, the forensic investigation of an individual clouds subsequent determinations. False criminal confessions and later reports from informants or witnesses set in motion a process that leads to incorrect conclusions.

The "chain of bias" is obvious in a review of 240 overturned police cases from 1992 to 2009 on the basis of DNA evidence.

Fifty-nine of these cases included false confessions by the suspect or by a suspected accomplice. The cases were more likely than others to involve incorrect findings by forensic investigators and were more likely supported by misguided or lying informants. Mistaken eyewitnesses appeared early in the investigation in three-quarters of the cases.

Of course we wonder why suspects confessed in the first place (duress, fatigue, misunderstanding, looking for the spot light?), but if the initial investigation points in the direction of guilt, subsequent evidence tends to support the initial findings.

In our own search for evidence of lying, we could also be biased by our initial impressions. If we conclude that the subject is a habitual liar, based on our first encounter, that impression may become self-reinforcing. It is therefore important to delay any conclusion and give the person the benefit of the doubt, and continue the search for multiple sources of relevant data.

** The study referred to in this discussion is from an "in press" article by Saul M. Kassin, Daniel Bogart, and Jacquline Kerner, *Confessions that corrupt: Evidence from the DNA Exoneration Case Files, Psychological Science* (In Press, 2012).

Linguistic Deviations among Psychopaths

Verbal expressions can reveal unusual patterns of word and sentence construction, such as these. In combination, these unusual language habits may point to a psychopathic constitution.

> Speaking in incoherent sentences.
> Repeating your words when answering a question.
> Avoiding direct answers to questions.
> Speaking in a monotonous cadence, jumping tone and pitch, quick changes in ideas.
> Excessive explanations for unusual behaviors.
> Using third-person descriptions (rather than committing to "I").
> Emphatic pronouncements ("No way I would do that").
> Use of definitive reactions to questions, such as "Never," "Of course not," "Certainly not," "Actually," "No, I did not." Avoidance of typical contractions, such as "I didn't do it."
> Leaving out pronouns as identifiers (he, she, it, etc.) in order to distance oneself from revealing self-incriminating information.
> Pausing mid-sentence, as if confused.
> Using sarcasm or humor to deflect listeners from self-incriminating data.
> Smiling at unusual times.

Showing verbal aggression or withdrawal if confronted with disbelief.

Researchers Jeffrey Hancock and Michael Woodworth (summarized at Huffingtonpost.com, 10–24 –2011) additionally report that psychopaths lack emotion in their characterizations and speak matter-of-factly to describe crimes they have committed.

In their study, 14 imprisoned psychopathic murderers, in contrast to 38 murderers who were not classified as psychopathic, used words such as "because" or "so that," to imply that the crime was an inevitable consequence of cause and effect circumstances. This is apparently a strategy to justify their behavior. The psychopathic population also used more "ums" and "uhs," indicating, perhaps, that they had difficulty retelling their crimes.

According to Hancock and Woodworth, the psychopaths seemed to operate on a primitive but rational level, avoiding all personal responsibility for their crimes.

What to Expect

The churning mind drives the pattern and cadence of written narratives and verbal expression. More than any other characteristic, linguistic qualities reveal the extent of psychopathic purpose – all processes are partially exposed through images from the psychopathic mind.

One's moral base and perceptions of the world are mirrored in writing and speech. In a real sense, people are what people think and how they express themselves. Words matter and cohesiveness of linguistic construction give us a view of how the brain works and the degree to which emotions participate in the drama of life.

These fundamental mental processes make it possible for us to assess the presence or absence of psychopathy, detect liars, measure the blunting of empathy, and foretell the weight of narcissistic ambitions. Thus far, linguistic analyses give us the edge over other measures of psychopathy. Eye movements, body language, and motor responses are far less reliable than words and sentence structure. They may add slightly to the credibility of our judgments, but nothing appears as reliable as what we hear and read. It is the constructed story line of the psychopath that is pregnant with information.

PROFIT AND LOSS ON A GIGANTIC SCALE

> A little cooling down of animal excitability and instinct, a little loss of animal toughness, a little irritable weakness and descent of the pain-threshold, will bring the worm at the core of all our unusual springs of delight into full view, and turn us into melancholy metaphysicians.
>
> WILLIAM JAMES, PSYCHOLOGIST

S. Nassir Ghaemi, MD and Professor of Psychiatry at Tufts University, writing in his recent book *A First Rate Madness* (Penguin, 2011), takes the unusual position that the best leaders in troubled times are often touched by madness. Ghaemi points to Winston Churchill, Mahatma Gandhi, and Abraham Lincoln (all with periodic depression and thoughts of suicide) as examples of outstanding leadership that lies quiescent in the disturbances of the brain. He asserts that someone who is mentally healthy "is insensitive to suffering" and therefore is unable to identify with the needs of the moment.

Accordingly, it is the off-centered, risk-taker, and deep seeker of change that explodes myths, defies history, ascends to power, and leads a nation out of darkness. Under the clouds of melancholy or narcissism and agitation, leaders – often troubled Machiavellians – embrace new ideas and often resolve major crises.

It is distressing to think that our cultural leaders may be mentally irresponsible. Ghaemi may have exaggerated the association between mental illness and leadership, but he does have a point. Accordingly, he believes that leaders touched by insanity toil in sadness when society is happy (*Wall Street Journal*, July 30/31, 2011) and only bloom under the weight of trauma. Not all do that, and as we have found; Machiavellian leaders ride the parallel rails of great success and imminent disaster.

As we witness in this chapter, history supports the notion that the Machiavellian personality is found disproportionately in the swirling circumstances of events, either to lead with wit and sword or collapse with failure and scorn. Harsh episodes, early poverty, loss of love, resentment, and unannounced bad luck fall to the unfortunate, but the consequences may ironically resonate across civilizations.

Never Waste a Perfectly Good Crises

Rahm Emanuel, then Chief of Staff at the White House and now Mayor of Chicago, realized the value of a crisis to galvanize the people to a purpose and to grease the skids that can drive a person to greatness. Rahm repeated this mantra in November of 2008 at a *Wall Street Journal* Forum: "You never want a serious crisis to go waste."

Indeed, crises have historically been the catalysts of greatness.

LEADERS BROUGHT TO POWER BY ADVERSITY	DRIVING FORCES OF CULTURAL STRESS
Demosthenes (330 BCC)	Athens threatened by expanding Macedon and encroaching Philip. He told the people that he was the single person who could bring victory to Athens.
Hannibal (218 BCC)	Carthaginian general delivered a monumental Speech to his army after crossing the Alps with 50,000 soldiers and 37

	elephants and entered Italy to attack the Romans.
Jonathan Edwards (1741)	The Great Awakening of religious fervor swept the American colonies. Edwards took up the challenge to unify its purpose and weed out the bad seeds that resisted his efforts.
Patrick Henry (1775)	Leader of the American Revolution who rallied the people with keen insight and absolute courage. He famously said: "Give me liberty, or give me death."
Susan B. Anthony (1873)	Against the background of the civil rights movement following the Civil War, she fought for women' suffrage and freedom from male abuse.
Winston Churchill (1940)	Warned England of the Nazi danger, fought brilliantly during WWII. Came to power during a deep economic depression.
Adolf Hitler (1938)	Sudden rise to power during an economic depression in Germany, prior to invasion of Poland and the start of WWII.
Franklin Delono Roosevelt (1933)	United States economic depression was in full Swing, facilitating his rise to power.
Douglas MacArthur (1880-1964)	Brought the United States through WWI, WWII and Korea. He was an incomparable general.
George S. Patton (1880-1945)	In large measure he was the Third Army general who destroyed the Nazi influence in Europe. His motto: "Kill the Bastards."

Not only did these individuals have the courage and temptation to assume leadership, they were all kissed by the gods with oratorical splendor. They rode the charismatic train to fame and promised an escape from darkness and the hope to emerge into light. "Our moment has come," they all announced in one way or another. They lived on threads of hope and thought in terms of revolution and victory in battle. They moved in circles of power, fame, and money.

It is a Faustian bargain between the commanding leader and their followers. The leader gives the people what they want to hear and believe, and the followers give up their individual freedom in order to serve the commander and the common path. The bond between "master" and "apostle" is strong, the leader knowing that the medium is the message – its content, its implementation, and its imperfections, or untruths, are unimportant.

For the common experience, the followers propel the leader to power, help the medium accomplish his or her goals, and protect the leader from criticism and bodily harm. The services that followers receive are of special status, retribution, and perhaps redistribution of wealth.

Great commanders exposed to the trembling and fear of their audiences are always at risk, and they may be cut down, either for what they represent, their ideology, or what they accomplish, or for the failures to produce, or for the crimes that they may commit. Economic and cultural demons stir the broth of the cauldron, and the questionable leaders float to the top.

The Generality of Greatness

The rise to greatness is not limited to political or military motivations but extends to our prodigious and brilliant playwrights, poets, literary giants, writers, scientists, religious leaders, and educators. In their particulars, they strive for greatness and flourish because of their aesthetic values, giving culture the soft lessons of humanity. Machiavellians, many, their personal lives are often filled with tragedies and lost opportunities.

Dr. Redfield Jamison, Professor of Psychiatry at the Johns Hopkins University School of Medicine, and herself a bipolar person, author of a famous book, *Touched with Fire: Manic-Depressive Illness and the Artistic Temperament* (Free Press Paperbacks, 1993), probes the artistic mind to show us in stark terms the self-consuming fire of artistic greatness and the artist's struggles for perfection. The numbers are daunting, as exemplified by the mental illness found among famous writers.

Lifetime Prevalence of Mental Illness Among Writers

Psychiatric Diagnosis	Writers (N = 30) %	Controls (N = 30) %
Any affective disorder	80	30
Any bipolar disorder	43	10
Alcoholism	30	7
Drug abuse	7	7
Major depre-ssion	37	17
Suicide	7	7
Schizophrenia	0	0

After Kay Redfield Jamison 1993,

The mortality rate for untreated manic depressives is higher than that for many types of heart condition and cancer. Poets are especially disposed toward mental disorders, many of which are fatal. Sylvia Plath (1932 – 1963), the victim of a grisly suicide, left us a portfolio of incredible poems and books. One stanza from *Death and Co.*, written about a year before her death, gives us a stark view of her thoughts.

> I do not stir.
> The frost makes a flower,
> The dew makes a star,
> The dead bell.
> The dead bell.
>
> Somebody's done for.

Artists and scientists travel in different outer circles of associates and conditions than do political and military aspirants, but their inner circles, the obsessions of the mind, are shared. They invariably live "outside the chicken coop," following their own dreams and avoiding the machinations of others. It's not easy to survive outside the chicken coop among the predators, but if anything is wired into the genotype, it is the reaching toward freedom and the dance for immortality. Many bear the same burden of insecurity, the need for fame and adulation, the belief in the perfectibility of humans (in a generic sense and not an individual sense), the narcissism of seeking, the belief in destiny, a reduced empathy for other humans, and the fear that death may be permanent. Nothing deflects their ambitions, and if all fails, they drink the hemlock.

The Capitalistic Marvel and the Psychopathology of Financial Leaders

When the rewards are greater – the grass is greener – the more likely male and female Machiavellians sniff out the trail of greatness. It is not merely chaos and the will to power that drive the Machiavellian, but also greed and the sense of invulnerability. Big business, including the corporations, large banks, non-democratic governments, and other competitive enterprises, often show an unusually large number of psychopaths with their hands on the throttle. For instance, Babiak and Hare (*Snakes in Suits: When Psychopaths go to Work*, Harpor, 2006) have data indicating that corporations have about three to four times the number of psychopaths working in the capitalistic system than expected by chance.

From the sidelines our lot in life is constant exposure to the whirling derby of mental deviations, the vacillating episodes of mob violence, the psychopathic ascension of tyrannical leaders, the self-centered callousness of genius, and the self-absorption of pompous asses. Be it sometimes we, that trample and trade, we must also deal with ourselves.

It is not difficult to respond to the Machiavellian version of a new leader, who may be tainted by madness, but offers a raw vision and a personal flair that can rally people when the world is crumbling all around. Observing a number of political seekers tells us that the psychiatrist S. Nassir Ghaemi is correct; it may take the touch of madness for someone working the high wire of fate to break through to a new and different level of understanding. The typical admonitions and cautions of old systems, stale political parties, former war heroes, and likely losers simply won't do. Folks are looking for the Churchills, the Lincolns, and the Gandhis for leadership, the roll of the dice. They are at first looking at the media, not the message. A candidate for political position may be a wobbly cannon, but some will believe that that dodging the cannonball is better than lobbing a small tennis ball toward the net. Somehow our genetic structure leads us to questionable individuals during periods of economic and social disruptions, and it gives us the courage to live outside the chicken coop and sample new possibilities. In the next few years we will see how willing people are to roll those dice.

One cannot usually tell when a Machiavellian will support our cultural values or go an independent way that we would like to avoid. Identifying a Machiavellian is the first step toward a decision, but the second step of giving or withholding support may be debatable in our minds. Let's be clear: we will never know for sure what the best approach is. The drawing out of the recent GOP primary election has given us detailed exposure to individual personalities, but in the end many voters still could not be sure of their choice. At some point, like the characters risking their lives in the movies, *Jackass*, voters just go for it. We hope for the best and go for the change. That's what life amounts to.

BLACKER THAN BLACK

We are not naïve enough to ask for pure man; we ask merely for men whose impurity does not conflict with the obligations of their job.

Jean Rostand
French biologist

Where there is no vision, the people perish.
BIBLE, HEBREW, PROVERBS 29:18
QUOTED BY J.F. KENNEDY ON THE EVE OF HIS ASSASSINATION

The Birth and Death of Hubris

Psychopaths forever are running freely through the business world, creating empires, building images, and utterly destroying the foundations of trade and commerce. From the chaos of destruction their profits skyrocket.

Slip-Ups and The Dangerous Mind

While the investors, consumers, and workers experience loses, the least-principled people rise to the top. I have watched the birth and death of many businesses, from corporations to small ventures, but claim no special knowledge about the details of many business declines. Nevertheless, the summaries tell the basic stories.

The rise and fall of the corporation Enron is a classic example of the warp-speed fraud that can both build incredible corporate giants and initiate activities that affect the lives of thousands of employees and hundreds of creditors. With lightning speed Enron rose as a model of business acumen and community excellence, only to collapse under the weight of corruption, fraud, and narcissism, ending in bankruptcy, prosecution, and shame.

Emerging in the 1990s as a prototype of modern corporate empires, with headquarters in Houston, Enron executives assumed that owning assets and manufacturing products were old-fashioned and unnecessary in the new-age of information flow and electronic management. The company would build an asset, such as a power plant, and almost simultaneously claim a profit on their books based on projected profits. When the revenue was less than expected the corporation transferred these assets to an off-the-books corporation and didn't report the loses on the Enron balance sheet.

The attitude of the CEOs Ken Lay and his successor Jeffery Skilling was that profits are a manifestation of accounting practices, not revenues. Schemes were devised by CFO Andrew Fastow to hide losses with the use of special purpose entities (SPE) and issue common stock to compensate for the losses. It was a Ponzi scam where profits were always assumed and losses were hidden until they could become profits. By October of 2001 the company posted its first quarter loss and closed its "Raptor" SPE so that it didn't have to issue 58 million shares of stock.

The practices of Enron finally triggered the attention of the Security and Exchange Commission (SEC), opening investigations that highlighted the dubious practices of Enron. A few days later Enron changed pension plan administrators, preventing employees from selling their shares in the company. It was a shock felt 'round the world.

The company was in free fall, and filed for bankruptcy in December of 2001. Prosecutors ended the charade and thousands of workers and creditors lost everything. Enron will go down in history as an example of greed and hubris in the corporate world, a symbol of glitzy psychopathy.

New World Psychopathy

The current counterpart to Enron is a new story of devastation centered in the financial heart of MF Global, a futures and commodities brokerage firm led by Jon Corzine, former top executive at Goldman Sachs and former New Jersey senator and governor. The depth of this fraudulent enterprise is yet to unravel.

A real rock and roll star on Wall Street, and a Democratic political insider, Jon Corzine assumed the top executive slot at MF Global in November, 2010. His job, apparently, was to return the firm to profitability by transforming MF Global into an investment bank and accelerating its proprietary trading.

At the point Corzine joined MF Global, the firm had around 36,000 accounts with $5.5 billion in funds. Quickly, however, with leveraged investments in European debt (Belgium, Italy, Spain, Ireland, and Portugal), large amounts of money simply disappeared – as much as $1.2 billion in customer money.

When MF Global declared a $191.6 million loss for the third quarter ending September 30, 2011, the news spooked investors and the credit rating of the company fell below investment grade. This sudden change of fortune initiated regulatory investigations by the FBI, the SEC, and the Commodities Trading Commission (CTC), forcing MF Global into bankruptcy. Approximately 1,066 employees are losing their jobs without access to severance pay, company benefits, and other financial perks.

No one knows where this is going. Yet, there is evidence of mismanagement, the mixing of segregated funds, and over-leveraged investments with margin calls. MF Global may have taken money from normal investment accounts to cover the margin calls and continue its commodity investments. It all looks like fraud on a gigantic scale, with the little guy again paying the price for the company's failure.

The full extent of the damage to investors, brokers, customers, taxpayers, and employees is yet to be tallied, and the blame hasn't been ascribed to illegal maneuvers by Jon Corzine or the traders involved, but the massacre has a familiar fishy odor. Parenthetically, Jon Corzine simply tells a Congressional investigative committee that he has no idea where all the money went. Shouldn't the top CEO know?

The debacle goes far beyond that of Enron, as billions of dollars are involved and the landslide consequences of self-destruction are almost too severe to measure. We'll keep our antenna up for further development.

Sunbeam in the Morning and Evening

In the free market environment companies may fail for a variety of reasons. They may be under- capitalized and cannot withstand economic downturns; they may lose out in the competition with other businesses; management may be inept or lack insight; changing market conditions may lower prospects of profits; or corruption from within or without may damage the company's ability to function.

The effects may be disastrous for the companies under pressure to succeed. Sometimes venture capitalists step in with money to stabilize the companies. At other times the companies may readjust their practices, downsize, or simply go out of business. Capitalism often dishes out tough lessons, and the ripple effects are long-lasting.

Among the most disastrous consequences for business are when corporate raiders "destroy companies in order to save them." The business may be forced to close, or downsize their activities, or they may be forced to merge with more successful firms. The companies may eventually be turned around or forced into bankruptcy.

Psychopathic personalities can be involved at any level of business. They are attracted to chaotic situations when assets are sold for pennies on the dollar, or they sometimes help to find ways to reestablish profitability in distressed environments. They also can cause disruption of orderly business activities and add to the list of problems. In fact, psychopaths may be the leading edge of both rebuilding or destroying companies

One of the worst examples of wholesale destruction is Sunbeam corporation, a well-known brand company that has produced electric home appliances since 1910. Their products include the Mixmaster mixer, the Sunbeam waffle iron, Coffee Master and the T20 toaster. Sunbeam, after going through hell, is now owned by Jarden Consumer Solutions. One of the most important divisions of Sunbeam is the Oster brand of appliances. Oster was acquired by Sunbeam in 1981.

Things went bad in 1986 when Sunbeam shareholders accused CEO Robert Buckley of misappropriating funds. According to the vivid story told by Jon Ronson (*The Psychopath Test*, 2011, Penguin Group) things were so bad that Buckley may have had a little security guy follow him around with a machine gun.

Buckley was the initial psychopath who brought Sunbeam to its ultimate end. He lived high as CEO, keeping a fleet of five jets for himself and his family, providing a $1 million apartment for his son, and charging the company $100,000 for wine. Can you believe it, the company was not making money and its decline was rapid?

Earlier, the company had been purchased by Allegheny International. Because of the disaster of Buckley and the stock market decline of October, 1987, Allegheny filed for Chapter 11 Bankruptcy. But the worst for Sunbeam was yet to come.

In 1996 Albert J. Dunlap (known as "chainsaw Al"), a wizard at turning failing companies around, was recruited as CEO of Sunbeam. In a short time, and with other acquisitions, Sunbeam rocketed to $52 a share, a sure sign that Dunlap had turned Sunbeam around. An internal investigation revealed, however, that Dunlap had cooked the books, and that Sunbeam was in severe crisis. Dunlap was fired. The SEC sued Dunlap, indicating that $60 million of the recovered profits of $189 million resulted from fraudulent accounting. The SEC fined Dunlap over $18 million and mandated that he never again head a company.

As part of Dunlap's plan of "reconstructing" Sunbeam, he closed plants in eight southern states, fired half of Sunbeam's 12,000 employees, and turned communities into ghost towns. Some towns that depended on Sunbeam for employment will never be able to make a comeback. Despite the fraud and callousness, Dunlap walked away with a $100 million plus severance pay – not a bad haul for Dunlap who only had to pay the SEC about $18 million.

Dunlap bought a lavish mansion in Florida surrounded by sculptures of predatory animals that Dunlap identifies with. He even published a book, appropriately titled *Mean Business* (1996, Crown Business). He is happy with his success and not displeased with his reputation as a company murderer. On his desk at home is a framed poem that guides his days.

"It wasn't easy to do
what he had to do.
But if you want to be
liked, get a dog or two."

The story is sad, but again shows us how a few psychopaths can cause inestimable damage and heartbreak. Incredibly Sunbeam, under the leadership of Jarden Corporation is continuing to grow brands and is predicted to be a good investment for low-risk earnings. Amazing.

The BS Psychopathic Test and Other Delights

According to comments by Clive R. Boddy (*The Corporate Psychopath,* Journal of Business Ethics, 2012), psychopaths that are elevated to power in financial corporations influence the moral climate of an entire organization. Financial giants may, in fact, deliberately choose the psychopathic personality for important positions, knowing that they will aggressively push the company agenda.

Ironically, Professor Robert Hare, a leading proponent of quantitative tests to identify psychopaths, and his colleague Dr. Paul Babiak, are designing a comparable test to identify psychopaths in business organizations. They call it the Business Scan, or the BS scan, for identification purposes.

The BS instrument will look for executive dysfunction, including:

> Those who have unusually high-dollar retirement plans, often with stock options.
> Evidence for previous SEC violations or investigations.
> Other CEO impressions of an individual's reputation.
> Evidence for living high on the hog.
> Ruthless cutting of employees.

The question I have is whether organizations will apply the BS evaluation for weeding out psychopaths or for attracting them for special positions? It will be interesting to see what happens.

In any case, there is sufficient evidence for the heavy influence of psychopaths in business atmospheres, as well as all other organized functions where opportunities beacon. We probably should keep in mind that psychopaths gravitate to position of authority wherever opportunities exist – not merely business. It happens with high frequency in social areas, educational circles, science, athletics, and government.

Howard Hughes Goes Rocket

I am impressed with Howard Hughes who understood how to balance personal interests with community service. His philanthropic interests benefited thousands. In 1953 Hughes launched the biomedical research center, the Howard Hughes Medical Institute in Chevy Chase, Maryland. The institute is dedicated to researching and eradicating all deadly diseases of mankind. Clearly these and other charities that Hughes supported benefited this country, but along the way he often used his community contributions (or promises) to deflect critics or legal investigations that might slow his other projects, such as buying up casinos and hotels and other real estate in Las Vegas.

> *"With each fortnight bringing a fresh report of some new Hughes contribution to the public welfare, it was none too surprising that the state legislature lost interest in conducting a serious investigation of concentrated ownership in the gaming industry. Once again, public relations triumphed." (p 308)*
> DONALD L. BARLETT AND JAMES B. STEELE, *HOWARD HUGHES: HIS LIFE AND MADNESS*, W.W. NORTON & CO., NEW YORK, 1979.

Hughes was touched by Machiavellian madness with high narcissism, low empathy, extreme sensation seeking, grandiose ideas, paranoia, obsessive compulsive behaviors, manic-depressive swings, and hypochondriac fears. He was also one of the world's wealthiest entrepreneurs, giving him the flexibility that can facilitate psychopathic activities.

The stories about his selfishness and peccadillos are legend, as are his aviator exploits, movie production, airline ownership, playboy pursuits, numerous near fatal airplane crashes, and, in the end, his reclusiveness and extreme disheveled condition.

By today's standards, Howard Hughes was not extremely wealthy, though he lived the part. The public exaggeration indicated that Hughes was worth from $1.5 billion to $2.5 billion. The best estimate is that he died with a fortune of at least $600 million and at most around $900 million. Author Bartlett and Steele put an interesting spin on his wealth, saying:

"If Hughes had invested the profits of the tool. Company, left to him by his father, in a passbook saving account, he would have died a richer man."

But that doesn't measure the character of the man. It was his legend that Hughes was obsessed with, the image of an untouchable genius whose influence reached around the world and is still influencing much of what we do, have, and aspire to. The list of his accomplishments, many pounded out from intimidation, massive spending, and political partnerships, are far too many to numerate or comprehend.

In just one of many regions of his influence, we can see the scope of his authority. It was Hughes's organization that placed communication satellites into orbit and linked the world in spectacular fashion. On June 1, 1966, the United States placed an unmanned Hughes Surveyor spacecraft on the moon, transmitted thousands of photographs back to earth and set the stage for the manned moon landing that made history.

The Navy's F-14 Tomcat jets were equipped with the sophisticated Hugh's weapon system, and the Phoenix missiles, also Hugh's products, that were guided to their targets by television for precision strikes on enemy targets.

The developments coming out of the Hughes Aircraft Laboratories changed the way we communicate, how we fight wars, and how we view our lives.

Howard Hughes was a bare-knuckle Machiavellian warrior who lacked empathy for most people but still affected their lives, with products and ideas that improved their futures. Almost like the Pharos of ancient Egypt, that used forced labor for creating lasting images of incomparable human achievements. Hughes, with genius and foresight, extended our impact on science, economics, and invention far beyond our wildest dreams. The question will always remain for anyone who builds new models of life and behavior, are the changes in our thinking and acting worth the heartbreak that was part of the necessary steps to achieve new forms and thinking?

Psychopathic, yes, genius beyond the ordinary, and aspirations and vision spinning through the planetary system and beyond, Howard Hughes, a physical and mental wreck of 90 pounds died April 5, 1976 on his last flight into Houston, giving us a legacy never matched and forever remembered. That's a Mach for you.

The Ponzi Scheme of Bernie Madoff

There was not enough money to go around, so the power investor Bernie Madoff took form the rich, gave them fraudulent reports of his investor success, and lived like a king.

Born April 29, 1938 in New York City he parlayed $5,000 earned as a lifeguard into one of the greatest fortunes ever. If we believe that the worst can only emerge from corporate fraud, and if corporations did not exist, life would be just great, then we should consider the mental landscape of Bernie Madoff.

Madoff had his Wall Street Connections, alright, but he was mainly an individual financial advisor that we might find in any money-making environment. Ending class differences would not end con jobs and mayhem; it would only change the nature of the psychopathy and the target of criminal interest . He is in this book because of the grandiose nature of his criminal strategies and his strange believability by hundreds of investors.

Moving up the social and educational ladder, Madoff began his study of law at Brooklyn Law School, and later began his own investment firm. With the help of his father-in-law he amassed an impressive client list of movie stars and other notables. He became famous for his reliable return of an annual rate of 10 percent on client investments. By the 1980s his firm accounted for up to five percent of the trading on the New York Stock Exchange.

Prospective clients came to him, almost begging to become a client. He made contacts on golf courses, in lavish restaurants, and as a result of business and social contacts. This was no ordinary con man. He was bright, sophisticated, well-mannered, and perfectly attired. He surrounded himself with symbols of wealth, including multi-million dollar houses for his families, and he groomed his image with care.

The money rolled in, but under pressure by the SEC he finally admitted to his sons that he had lost $50 billion of his investors' money. He was imprisoned and pled guilty to 11 felony counts, security fraud, money laundering, false statements, perjury, and false filings with the SEC, and theft from an employee benefit plan.

About $170 billion moved through Madoff's account but the financial statements showed a total of only $65 billion, indicating that he had lost more than a $100 billion of his clients' money. Madoff was found guilty on all substantive counts and was sentenced to 150 years in prison, and that's where he is today.

There is no need to list his losing clients. We only need to indicate that hundreds of superstar clients were involved, losing billions of dollars.

The names covered 162 pages of clients, ranging from major banks, investment firms, golf courses, Hollywood stars and directors, senators, governors, baseball owners, insurance companies, universities, religious foundations, business executives, and many other well-known celebrities. Profits were exaggerated in reports to clients and losses hidden behind accounting practices.

Others may have known about the Ponzi scam and even helped perpetuate the prestigious image of Bernie Madoff. The scheme was vast and eluded the scrutiny of the SEC for decades, making it difficult even now to get an accurate accounting.

One thing is clear. Bernie Madoff was a psychopathic crook of major proportions, putting forth an image of wealth and success – narcissistic with the best and callous with the worst. This story is a unique in its pattern of behavior but not in the underpinnings of the psychology behind the crimes. It makes us wonder if there can ever be adequate checks against psychopathic assaults on well-meaning investors.

The Good, the Better, the Beautiful

We've seen the worst of the worst, CEOs, management teams, and financial advisors, as well as those who may be Machiavellian but nevertheless sometimes meritorious in their overall agenda of building and developing. Many are responsible for damaging companies for their own benefit. Of course, there are also bad economic policies, heavy taxes, and over enthusiastic regulations that can destroy companies and people.

One thing should be evident: the United States capitalistic system has always been strong and beneficial, and still is, but it must be protected if it is to continue. Despite the Enrons of the world, the Medoffs, and the Dunlaps, despite government intervention in private enterprise, and despite harsh economic environments, the overall record of U.S. businesses is stellar.

The market tends to weed out the bad apples; the successful businesses normally prevail. For every incompetent or psychopathic leader or CEO, there are hundreds of outstanding and honest business leaders. These individuals, as did Steve Jobs, and generally Howard Hughes, pursue innovation and excellence, and live exemplary lives. Of course, they often make millions and even billions of dollars, and they sing their own song, but they regularly reinvest their assets, support communities in which they live, and work hard to improve their companies and the world around them. They also, not so incidentally, support the economy, employ millions, pay the majority of taxes, support the arts, and act as the intellectual backbone of our country.

Those who would destroy capitalism and advocate socialism diminish all of us with their destructive envy and greed. Capitalism hands out difficult lessons and uncertainty, but it is at the same time the consistent path to prosperity and opportunity. It is better to aspire than expire, and better to try, than die in poverty and socialistic darkness.

I add a note of optimistic reality by pointing to a few of the many companies in the United States that, for a *minimum* of 25 years, have shown significant profits for investors and serve as a network of entrepreneurial excellence. Some of these companies actually have a history of over one hundred years of serving our needs and desires. My short list is from a much longer list of S&P stocks called Dividend Aristocrats that have shown a minimum of 25 years of annual increases in dividend payouts to investors, and have excellent records of capital gains. Thousands of people have retired rich by steady investments in these or similar companies.

United States Corporations (Dividend Aristocrats) *

Company Symbol	Company Name	Recent Dividend Yield [%]	Payout Ratio [%] **	EPS ***
XOM	Exon Mobil Corp	2.40	30.75	10.55
WMT	Wal-Mart Stores	2.26	28.97	10.15
MCD	McDonald's Corp	3.19	47.91	10.05
ADM	Archer Daniels Midland	1.99	21.25	7.80
ABT	Abbott Laboratories	3.71	56.29	9.70
JNJ	Johnson & Johnson	3.49	41.71	6.27
PG	Proctor & Gamble	2.98	48.74	8.61
KMB	Kimberly-Clark Corp	4.18	57.84	7.63
KO	The Coca-Cola Co	2.70	52.67	8.33
ED	Consolidate Edison Inc	4.79	69.30	4.38

*http://scottsinvestments.blogspot.com/2010/12/

** Payout ratio is the ratio between dividend paid divided by share price, expressed as a percent.

*** EPS (earning per share) is the projected stock earnings in the next five years.

These Dividend Aristocrats encourage long-term non-speculative investing in companies with lasting achievement, sound financial policies, and sensitivity to peoples' needs. Rather than destroying the fundamental structure of the free enterprise system, one could accomplish a great deal by attempting to duplicate the successful investment models we now have. One can never anticipate future returns in any system perfectly, but historical reliability of companies providing basic products that everyone needs is just about as good as it gets. Even in rough economic times these companies have a distinct advantage over companies that cater to short-term social trends or pay no dividends at all.

Prophetically, investors should monitor stock performance and not fall in love with a particular stock that may disappoint. If the stock performance deteriorates one need not ride it down – one can find a new mount, build a diversified stable of mounts that can serve changing needs. It comes down to deciding how much risk an individual is willing to take and how one can protect investments. The S&P Dividend Aristocrats have many advantages but should not dictate lives.

The free market offers individuals opportunities and choices. History does matter, and the corruption of the market by psychopaths and cynics need not interfere with individual goals of independence, prosperity, and morality. There is no way to build economic organizations that absolutely are perfect in function, but we can concentrate our investments where the record of performance indicates suburb management and responsible citizenship. We have to exert care, of course, and be willing to risk what we can afford to lose.

The greatest slip-up that most of us experience is to believe that the mind looking at us over the table or from across the street is not dangerous. Mostly, we believe that because it is usually true; we experience no ill effects. Moreover, we tend to see ourselves in other people, believing that there is goodness in most people. We draw on our experiences and give others the benefit of any doubt.

Any, why not? We would rather take a few chances, and be wrong once in a while, rather than walk constantly with paranoia. Mistakes are made, slip-ups happen, but life's tunes are not always melodious. It's just part of a game that has been with us since our early first steps in Africa.

There is a middle ground, where we show reserve and seek assurances before we commit to an idea or a person. Perhaps, the best advice for someone who is unsure of another is to proceed in slow motion, remain open for possibilities, and note reactions, and test for glimpses of reality.

Given time, and with patience, most of us can separate the interesting mind from the dangerous mind. Hopefully, the slip-ups will be few and without lament.

Throughout our seeking and screening of information we remember that the psychopath is narcissistic, charming, and disarming, but also full of stories and prevarications, a combination of traits that can cause him or her to skid into a revelatory slip-up. The game, then, is up, until the psychopath finds another game.

THE DISCONTENT OF KNOWING

The chemistry of dissatisfaction is the chemistry of some marvelously potent tar. In it are the building stones of explosives, stimulants, poisons, opiates, perfumes and stenches.

Eric Hoffer
U.S. philosopher

"We are wasted," Don murmured, looking over the massive destruction of the world's greatest city. "Yeah," Bill replied in a hushed voice. "But it was one hell of a ride." Bill handed his last bit of food to his mutt dog Phineas, and motioned for Don to follow. "Ever been to Georgia?" he asked, but got no reply. "Well, that's where we're going. There's probably some good water in those mountains, and food. We can set up camp there and think about things, sort of start again." Off the three went as strangers in a strange land.

An Evolutionary Farewell

In this chapter we file our last report on the dangerous mind, probing deeper for causes and at last turning to circles of history for understanding and a look into the future, a future where all the switches seem set for total destruction and final longing. Our search for resolution will end there, on the circle of fate.

Psychopaths are mainly born, not made, suggesting that there may have been selective forces early in our evolution to preserve and exaggerate some of our survival and reproductive traits. Once in place as critical advantages, hard-core psychopathic traits are difficult to modify. If recurring traits increase reproductive success, as I believe, there is less selection against their presence. Given the overwhelming concentration of evolutionary forces, key behaviors have a strong resistance to change. Psychoanalysts and psychological therapists, who want to believe that behaviors of psychopaths can be unlearned, might as well look for other work.

Of course, events can increase or decrease psychopathy, suggesting a reasonable amount of environmental influence. But the modification of psychopathic behaviors does not necessarily suggest that the major personality traits can be eliminated. Young males are more likely to be swept up in the sensations of risk-taking, or be caught in the excitement of mob destruction or revolution, or be drawn easily into the embrace of aggressive ideologies. As they mature and age, the desires for anarchy and revolution fade into the shadows of life. It would appear, therefore, that psychopathic behaviors seem like passing fancies – just kid stuff.

But another lesson gives a different impression. Psychopaths have a genetic nature that drives them toward risk-taking, chaos, and political destruction. They are more at home in mobs, in social revolutions, and in authoritarian politics. We shouldn't be misled to assume that chaos, mobs, revolutions, money, and politics *cause* psychopath, and if the worst doesn't happen the psychopathic urges fall like autumn leaves. It may be more generally true that psychopaths become participants in ongoing upheavals, rather than the reverse. It is among those of like emotions that they seek their advantage.

The psychopath has a genetic preparedness to respond to the call of novel, chaotic, and opportunistic environments – like the moth drawn into the danger of the candle flame. Bad behaviors may fade as opportunities vanish and as age writes over every journey, but the motivations for crime, aggression, and evil never leave the mind.

This is not to suggest that all individuals who might be caught up in the enchantment of mobs or non-traditional political movements are psychopathic – not at all – but, rather, that psychopaths are disproportionately represented among these groups. They go where the action is. In short, we should not confuse environmental modification of behavior with instinctive attraction to special environments. Perhaps looking back in history will reveal our true destiny.

The Circle of Fate

History did not always have an esteemed position in the catalogue of human affairs. Aristotle voiced his opinion:

"Poetry is something more philosophic and of graver import than history, since its statements

are of the nature of universals, whereas those of history are singulars."

He believed that all events were unique, never repeating. All was earth, air, water, and fire – variable and of momentary importance – not the atmosphere for reflection on the circles of the past.

The gate to the infinite past was opened by Greek Herodotus in the fourth century BCE. According to the historian Daniel Boorstin, Herodotus "was a force in the Ionian Enlightenment in which Greek philosophy and literature first developed." Herodotus reached backward for remembrances, recording for future generations his interpretation of the Persian War waged from 499 to 449 BCE. But the short breadth of inquiry told him nothing about history's resemblances over long periods of time.

Thucydides, an Athenian citizen and general, and designated as the original political scientist, pursued the new historical path opened by Herodotus. As a general and student of the Peloponnesian wars, he realized that human nature was constant even as the wars ebbed and flowed, as if every memory was hungry for rebirth. This may have been the first indication that historical events move in cycles and human glory and peril follow rather than drive history.

Slip-Ups and The Dangerous Mind

Historian Niall Ferguson points to an early cyclical hypothesis. In Book VI of the Greek historian Polybius' *Histories*, it is said that political stages occur over long periods of time and then repeat themselves, as follows:

1. Monarchy
2. Kingship
3. Tyranny [stage of the psychopath?]
4. Aristocracy
5. Oligarchy
6. Democracy
7. Ochlocracy (mob rule, and an important stage of the psychopath)

Other philosophers, sociologists, and historians embraced the concept of the "circle of fate," observing that empires inevitably rise and fall, and never remain constant. More recently scientists direct their statements to *time* as the conduit of growth and decline, mirrored in the heavens by planetary and galactic motion, in the layers of fossilized bones in earth's sediments, with ocean-bottom faults that spread and unite continents, by climate change, and the seasons of birth and death, the ticking of our atomic calculators, and the calendar of our days. Within us, too, physiology moves in clock-like fashion, affecting our sleep, hormones of behavior, neurological bases of mental states – all nested in mysterious waves of repetition.

We evolved traits to match the cycles of nature, but we have never overcome them. The best we have done is to minimize their consequences by building barriers and shelters, growing, processing, and storing needed materials, constructing tools and weapons, banding together in defense of tribes, educating ourselves in lit corners, and, it might be argued, developing myths and religions to explain change. We know little of the mechanisms of cyclic variations, but the intuitive traces of cycles seem to jog our archetypical memories from time to time, providing biological messages of our evolutionary responses to change.

The psychopath is one of the few who believes that natural cycles can be chained to our needs, but others that investigate cycles are delighted if they can only measure their rhythm. The greatest ancient philosopher, Plato, had the idea that there is an inevitable decline of all political systems. He was named by the philosopher of science, Karl R. Popper, the patron saint of "historicism," appealing to the pessimistic belief that history is governed by unalterable rules of the universe, and man is not free to shape his own destiny.

Yet it was Plato who also believed that a utopia could be built and sustained against cyclical forces if only we harness and breed just and impartial leaders (Philosopher Kings) who could keep things right through rational thoughts and actions, thus serving the communal needs of the masses.

Plato, delivering his notions through his old mentor Socrates, put forward that truth and goodness "[are] like the sun, the source of light that enables people to see." For Plato, knowledge accrues as a straight line from unenlightened imagining of surroundings of purely abstract reasoning, where sensory impressions disappear and the mind – clear and clean – does all the thinking. The leaders of utopia, the Philosopher Kings, can be trained during their formative years for their key functions and obligations, beginning their rule at age 50, thus binding the community together (as an impenetrable union) that can withstand the strong cyclical force of destruction. His notions became dogma. Man could overcome worldly and wily forces.

Dogma rarely survives, however, Kings falter, governments are cleansed by revolution or deterioration, presidents are overthrown, die, or out-voted, and demography, disease, and destruction ride like wild horses over the land. Time is the savior, it is believed; time is the reaper, others say, and all things change, including the number and strength of the psychopath.

The Cycle of Psychopathic Tyrany

From Europe to the Middle East and beyond to the United States, the streets are littered with psychopathic visions, their numbers seem to increase daily.

We know, too, with certainty that there was a time when psychopaths were sparse and revolutions infrequent. We believe, too, that the present chaos, while thick with portent, cannot last. It either initiates the collapse of our civilization, or ushers in a new birth of discovery and civility. The question is, can history point us to the causes of cycles and illuminate the cyclical change of psychopathy? Possibly.

Thomas Cole's five stunning paintings of the rise and fall of civilization, *The Course of Empire*, illuminate the emergence, flowering and fall of psychopathy in five sequential oil paintings. The literary inspiration for his paintings in the years 1833-1836 was Lord Byron's *Childe Harold's Pilgrimage* written between 1812 and 1818. Keep in mind that the literary and artistic insights into the cycles of life occurred in the early to middle 19th Century, decades ahead of scientific studies of cyclical behavior. Cole quoted a verse from Byron's Canto IV, setting the stage for his artistic representation of the cycle of civilization.

> *"There is the moral of all human traits; Tis but the same rehearsal of the past. First freedom and then Glory – when that fails, Wealth, vice, corruption – barbarism at last. And History, with all her volumes vast, Hath but one page . . ."*

Each of the five paintings depicts the world at the mouth of a great river beneath a rock precipice during the rise or setting of civilization. The first painting, *The Savage State*, shows the dawning of a stormy day, with a hunter clad in skins moving rapidly through the wilderness pursuing a deer. Canoes paddle up the river. On the far side is a clearing with wigwams around a fire, the place where a city will emerge in later paintings.

In the second painting, *The Arcadian or Pastoral State*, the stormy sky has cleared and the morning is a day in spring or early summer. The perspective changes but the crag with the boulder is still in view. Much of the wilderness has been replaced by settled lands with plowed fields and lawns visible. We can see plowing, boat-building, dancing, and herding of sheep. There seems to be a man with a stick, apparently working out a geometric problem. In general, the painting reflects an idealized, pre-urban ancient Greece.

The third painting, midway in the cycle of civilization, depicts the same area, but one changed in major ways. *The Consummation of Empire* shows a glorious summer day. The river valley is now covered with colonnaded marble structures, where steps run down into the water. Buildings and towers dominate the scene. Lateen sails are seen on the sea beyond. A joyous crowd throngs the balconies, dressed as scarlet-robed king or general. Fountains gush. It looks like the pinnacle of Roman civilization

The fourth painting, *Destruction* is the one that describes the assumption of power and destruction by invading psychopaths. A tempest brews in the background; a fleet of enemy warriors has overcome the city's defense and the invaders burn pillage, rape and kill the city's inhabitants. The scene is perhaps suggested by the Vandal sack of Rome in 455.

The fifth painting, Desolation, shows the Roman city years after the sacking. The city is in the livid light of a dying day – dark and brooding – the landscape is returning to wilderness and no humans are visible. The broken remains of the city emerge from beneath a mantle of trees, ivy, and other overgrowth. The arches of a shattered bridge and the columns of the temple are still visible, with a single column reflecting the haunting glory of civilization. The sunrise of the first painting is replaced by a pale sheen of moonlight reflecting in the ruined ashes and shards of civilization.

Edward Gibbon (1737-1794). Oswald Spengler (1880-1936), Arnold Toynbee (1889-1975), Pitirim Sorokin (1889-1968) and other great early thinkers, historians, and philosophers understood that no matter what we do, where we live, and the gods that we worship, there is a pattern of change in all great empires and small hamlets that informs us that civilizations often move from simple to complex, savagery to law-abiding, hunting and gathering to agriculture and large cities, and superstition to science, only to find that they collapse under their own weight, population increases, or invasion from without, and seem ready to repeat the entire cycle. The inevitability of cycles makes one puzzle as to why Progressive ideologists stand on the principles that man can perfect himself, that a classless society is possible, and that a utopia can be built on enforced communal good and sacrifice.

To those insights we can add the proposition that the rise and fall of psychopathic destruction moves along these same axes, increasing with the aggregation and consummation of civilization, exploding against the complexity of city states, and falling with the destruction of civilization and the resetting of the small tribal groups pursuing game, fishing, and gathering edible foods from the ground and naturally growing environments.

Our way of life today seems poised on the edge of survival in a complex civilization that is under increasing threat and violence by psychopaths (Thomas Cole's paintings three and four, respectively) with no obvious way to change the course of history. It appears that the cycle of fate is turning faster and faster with nations and civilizations crumbling within view and on a time-span that is astonishing. Rome fell within five decades, The British Empire vanished in two decades from 1945 to 1965, Nazi Germany fell within a single decade, the Soviet Union crumbled beginning in 1991 and was complete within a few years, Japan crashed as a contender on the world stage in less than a decade, and the countries of the Middle East are falling like dominos. The entire face of Europe seems to be in free-fall; emerging nations are quickly moving through their productive peaks, and China is beginning to strain under the pressures of internal conflict and economic peaks of demands and uncertainties. And the United States, from the perspective of some, is sliding into an unrecoverable depression and assault by foreign and internal psychopaths ready to destroy every institution. Hopefully, we can restrain the worst, reverse course, and not have to hoof it to the mountains and streams of Georgia with Don, Bill, and the mutt dog Phineas.

. . . until we meet again . . .

Proof

Made in the USA
Charleston, SC
21 May 2012